JAPAN

KUSAKABE KIMBEI *Buddhist Priest*, 1880s.
Albumen Print, 21.4 x 27.5 cm.

KUSAKABE KIMBEI   *Samurai Group*, 1890s.   Albumen Print, 20 x 27 cm.

JAPAN

PHOTOGRAPHS

1854 - 1905

For: Giles — a day in the country...

10.16.93.

Edited and with a historical text by
Clark Worswick

Introductory Essay by

Peter Grilli

Director of Education

Japan Society, Inc.

A Pennwick Book • Published for the Japan House Gallery and
The American Federation of Arts

ACKNOWLEDGEMENTS

Appreciation is extended to the following institutions and individuals who made collections available for the preparation of this book: the Library of Congress, Prints and Photographs Division; Richard Pare, the Peabody Museum of Salem, Massachusetts; the Smithsonian Institution; the Museum of Natural History, and Daniel Wolf.

I wish to acknowledge with gratitude the help and support of a small group of dedicated collectors of nineteenth-century Japanese photography who made this exhibition possible: Lawrence and Martha Friedricks (New York), Takeichi Ishiguro (Tokyo), Harry Lunn, Jr. (Washington), Arthur and Marilyn Penn (New York), Howard and Jane Ricketts (London), and Ichiro Ueno (Tokyo). In addition I wish to thank Rand Castile, Donald Richie, Eric Klestadt, Bill Jay, John Rosenfield, Porter McCray, Allen Wardwell, Chang-su Houchins, and Peter Grilli, who assisted greatly with the oftentimes difficult problem of defining the Meiji period.

Hiroaki Sato made a substantial contribution to a Western appreciation of photography in nineteenth-century Japan by transliterating complicated Japanese photographic chronologies into English. Both Victoria Wilson and Robert Gottlieb, at Alfred A. Knopf, have made an important contribution to the field of photography, and to the appreciation of the medium as an art, by seeing this publication through. Finally, I wish to thank Marilyn Penn, who devoted many months of work to the book in many stages as collaborator and editor.

Clark Worswick

The Japan House Gallery and The American Federation of Arts are pleased to present the exhibition "Japan: Photographs 1854–1905" and this book, which serves as well as the catalogue of the exhibition. After its initial installation at Japan House in the winter of 1979–1980 the exhibition will travel to museums throughout the United States under the auspices of the AFA.

We would like to express our thanks to Mr. Clark Worswick whose important work in the field of nineteenth-century photography is here extended to include the especially rich treasures of Japan. To our knowledge this is the first exhibition and publication in the West to treat the subject in depth.

We thank Mr. Francis Tenney of the Japan-United States Friendship Commission and his staff for generously assisting in the development of the exhibition and publication of this book. Mr. Tenney's interest and encouragement did much to make this project a reality. We are honored and pleased that the National Endowment for the Arts, too, provided substantial funding for the project.

Nineteenth-century Japan is nowhere better seen than in these photographs of men and ladies, actors and samurai on the roads they traveled, towns they inhabited, and houses they built. The pictures are still and from another time, but they speak strongly, not to the curious nor of the quaint, but of the singleness of a people at the moment of their opening up to the West.

Rand Castille
Director,
Japan House Gallery

Wilder Green
Director,
The American Federation of Arts

Library of Congress Cataloging in Publication Data Main entry under title:

Japan, photographs, 1854-1905.

1. Japan—Description and travel—1801-1900—Views.

2. Japan—History—19th century—Pictorial works.

I. Worswick, Clark.

DS809.J4 1979   952.03'022'2   79-2215

ISBN 0-394-50836-X

First Edition   Manufactured in the United States of America

Contents

The Meiji Period and Japan's Response to the West.

Viewed from the last quarter of the twentieth century, the events taking place in Japan in the latter half of the nineteenth may seem somewhat diminished in drama or historical magnitude. Can anything really compare, we may wonder, to the upheavals and transformations of Japan in our present era, most especially to her miraculous recovery from total devastation to a position of extraordinary international influence in the mere quarter-century following World War II? And historical hindsight, too, tends to lend an inescapable sense of inevitability to occurrences that in their own time must have seemed radical departures from the expected or the predictable. To some historians, the opening of Japan to international intercourse in 1853–54 and the subsequent technological and cultural modernization are merely the logical ramifications of European industrialization and the extension of the worldwide forces of capitalism and imperialism.

Nonetheless, Japan's nineteenth-century transformation is one of the miracles of modern history, and when we make the effort to view it in its own frame of reference we can only be astounded at the rapidity and the extent of the cultural changes that took place. A few historical milestones will suffice to indicate the remarkable speed of the transformation.

In 1854, a miniature steam locomotive brought by Commodore Perry as a gift to the Japanese Emperor with whom he was determined to negotiate treaties of diplomatic and commercial relations delighted the Japanese by its novelty. Dignified samurai threw all caution to the winds and rode recklessly on this remarkable Western toy, the likes of which they had never seen before. Less than two decades later, rail service was inaugurated between Tokyo and Yokohama, and in equally short order was extended to most other major Japanese cities. In 1854, the Japanese negotiators were powerless to resist Perry's demands that they open their country to the West; their domestic politics were in a shambles, their military apparatus hopelessly outdated, and the Shogun's bankrupt government was threatened with all manner of civil disorder. By 1873, the nation was unified under an energetic new administration and was powerful enough to launch overseas military expeditions to assert its will over China and Korea. And within a brief five decades after Perry's arrival, Japan had defeated Russia in battle, demonstrating to the world that she had joined the small circle of powerful industrial nations. In 1853, no more than a handful of people in the entire country were familiar with a foreign language, and the negotiations were hampered by the clumsy necessity of translating from Japanese to flawed Dutch to English and vice-versa. Again, within a mere two decades, hundreds of European books of all languages and subject matter had been translated into Japanese, equally large numbers of Japanese were enrolled in universities abroad, and thousands more were studying at home with European and American teachers, experts, and advisors.

Such feats of modernization cannot be accomplished overnight (except, perhaps, in Japan) or in isolation from one another. The building of a railroad system depends not only on an ability to lay track or build a locomotive, but on a myriad of interlocking technologies: an understanding of engineering, a source of raw materials and the ability to refine and transform them, a knowledge of geography and an ability to use surveying instruments accurately, etcetera. That such technologies and the scientific expertise underlying them were mastered so rapidly and skillfully is eloquent testimony to the irrepressible curiosity of the Japanese modernizers, to their sharp intelligence, and to their fierce determination to transform their society in order not to be left powerless and subjugated by the more advanced nations of the West.

The processes of cultural change, once set in motion, would leave no aspect of Japanese life unaffected. Eating habits, dress, architecture, manufacturing, civil administration and legal systems, scholarly and literary writing, domestic and international communications, art and music —everything was caught up in the whirlwind onslaught of modernization.

How was Japan's thoroughgoing transformation accomplished so rapidly? Why was she able to resist the total domination by alien imperialists that had victimized China,

and why was her response to the West unique among Asian nations? What were the cultural and psychological benefits and costs to her people? The answers to these questions and the vital historical drama that lies behind them can only be hinted at in the few pages available here. But some generalizations and some historical background are necessary before turning to the splendid photographs that illustrate specific images of Japan during the *Bakumatsu* (the period from about 1840–1860 known as the "twilight of the Tokugawa Shogunate") and the Meiji years.

It would be a gross oversimplification to imply that Japan's political, economic, and cultural modernization began overnight with the arrival of Commodore Perry's Black Ships in 1853, or with the creation of the Meiji government in 1867. The two-and-a-half preceding centuries, during which Japan was effectively isolated from the rest of the world by the exclusionist policies of the Tokugawa Shogunate, were hardly the static, calcified era that they have sometimes been described. True, under the long Tokugawa peace the tempo of innovation may have slowed somewhat from the years of civil warfare, the attempts at overseas expansion, and the interactions with European soldiers, traders, and missionaries in the sixteenth century. And in retrospect, Tokugawa time must certainly seemed to have moved slower than Meiji time. But the long period of stability under centralized Tokugawa rule permitted significant population growth and urbanization, innovation in agricultural techniques, and a high degree of domestic commercial activity. Furthermore, as a by-product of the limited trade carried on with the Chinese and Dutch at Nagasaki, enough information about European science entered Japan to encourage the curiosity of *Rangaku* ("Dutch learning") scholars, who struggled to keep abreast of Western medicine, physics, geography, optics, botany, and other natural sciences. Even the traditionalist Tokugawa government recognized the need to study the West, and in 1856 established the *Bansho Shirabeshō*, an agency to collect, translate, and analyze European books and documents on a great variety of subjects. Thus, a small foundation for Western learning had been laid prior to the Meiji period, and when full intellectual intercourse with the West was finally allowed there were numerous Japanese scholars avid to pursue European science and technology as far as they were able.

The Meiji Restoration of 1867, in which the central governing authority was wrested from the Tokugawa Shogunate and re-established in the name of the Emperor, was the result of a broad range of forces: intensifying pressures for greater access to Japan by European nations which the Shogunate was powerless to resist, conflict and rivalry among several powerful *han* or feudal domains that had nursed their resentment of the Tokugawa overlords for 250 years, the impoverishment of the samurai class whose military vocation had weakened under the long peace, and the development of a money economy and the enrichment of intrepid, innovative urban merchants who, though at the bottom of the hierarchical social scale, held the samurai as well as the Shogunate itself in debt. By the middle of the nineteenth century, the *Bakufu* (as the Tokugawa government was called) was financially, spiritually, and administratively bankrupt, and some form of major change could not have been long postponed. That it came in the form of an imperial restoration was far from predictable, however, and was due to an extraordinary combination of radical and reactionary forces. The use of the ancient im-

perial institution as the vanguard for revolutionary political and social innovation remained characteristic of the curious give-and-take of liberal and traditionalist impulses throughout the Meiji period.

One of the first public pronouncements of the youthful Emperor Meiji, acting as the mouthpiece of the Satsuma and Choshu samurai who engineered his accession to power in 1867, was the Imperial Charter Oath of April, 1868. In this simple but highly charismatic utterance was the motivation for all subsequent modernization: the Japanese people were called upon to unite in carrying out the administration of the new state, all individuals would be allowed to pursue freely their own callings, and all evil customs of the past were to be abandoned in favor of the "just laws of Nature." Most significantly, the Charter Oath promised that "Knowledge would be sought throughout the world so as to strengthen the foundations of imperial rule." This final article not only undercut the xenophobia with which Japanese nationalists had resisted the incursions of foreign diplomats and traders, but also threw open the gates of Japan to all manner of foreign customs and technology. Thus were the Japanese people given official sanction to launch the vigorous process of modernization that left no one's life unaffected. Most of the innovations were practical and clearly beneficial: telegraph communications, parliamentary institutions, newspapers, educational reforms of every conceivable sort, dietary changes, industrial expansion, and on and on and on. Some changes were motivated simply by vanity, however, and provoked ridicule not only by Western observers but by sensitive Japanese as well: such were the dark, uncomfortable Western rooms—complete to the last antimacassar—that wealthy Japanese built on to their homes, or the masquerades and fancy-dress balls at the famous Rokumeikan ("Deer Cry Pavilion") built in Tokyo in 1883 as a sort of club where the most *à la mode* of the Tokyo aristocracy could gather to display their latest Western affectations of dress and manners.

Any superficial description of a vital moment in history tends to give a distorted quality of uniformity to the picture. Innovation and modernization in Meiji Japan was not an orderly process in which all Japanese participated with unanimous zeal and enthusiasm. The period was plagued (or enriched) by conflicting motivations, political rivalries, and highly divergent philosophies of what the "new Japan" should look like. As the xenophobic nationalists of mid-century came to recognize the fruitlessness of their initial determination to "respect the Emperor and expel the foreigners," they adopted widely varying attitudes for reckoning with the Western presence in Japan. Many espoused a philosophy of "Eastern ethics and Western science" by which the advanced technologies of Europe and America might be imported and adopted only insofar as they did not tarnish the superior spirit of the Japanese soul. If there was any overriding intellectual unity among the Meiji modernizers it might be summarized by a slogan to which nearly all subscribed: *fukoku kyōhei* or "enrich the nation and strengthen the military." Modernization and Westernization were advocated as national goals not so much because of their own inherent worth but rather as techniques by which Japan could eventually assert her autonomy and free herself from fears of domination by the industrial nations of the West. Japanese who forsook their kimono for European dress and who affected an enthusiasm for the taste of beef could claim that they were doing so in order to convince the Westerners of Japan's civilized attainments. And motivating the transformation of the educational system and the creation of a legal code were the desire to demonstrate Japan's social and intellectual equality and her determination to remove the oppressive unequal treaties that cast her in an inferior position to the Western nations.

This essay has attempted to paint, in very broad strokes indeed, an impression of the era in which the fascinating photographs in the present collection were taken. It would be a mistake, however, to view the photographs as no more than a series of illustrations of historical points. They are not documents but rather the creations of artists playing with light and shadow and composition and design. The lovely light that they cast on nineteenth-century Japan is not a spotlight marking the great actors or events on the stage of history, but rather a diffused glow through which the viewer can admire the style and tone of the period as a whole. The "facts" are there too, to be sure, but one must peer carefully at the pictures to pick them out: the gas lights and English shop signs in the street scenes are clues to social innovations, as is the Western garb worn by some of the portrait subjects and the presence of foreign visitors in some of the photographs of famous places. The Japanese dandy, seated at a restaurant table and ordering what must be a very authentic European meal (Plate 46), illustrates brilliantly the silliness with which some Japanese discarded their traditional customs and affected Western manners. The frequently reproduced portrait of the Emperor Meiji (Plate 41), taken in 1872 by Uchida Kyuichi, is a clear statement of all the modernizing passion of the period. Although little individual personality shines through this portrait, the externals carry the full message: the nineteen-year-old Emperor in the fifth year of what was to be a forty-five year reign, sits with hair trimmed in the Western manner, wearing pants and a military jacket ornamented with gold braid, looking for all the world like a European prince; the face alone indicates that the subject is Japanese, but the setting, pose, and all aspects of his appearance are thoroughly Western.

Many of the photographs in this collection offer little or no hint at all of the dramatic Westernizing forces that were sweeping the world of Meiji Japan. It is curious that the Western photographers—Felix Beato, A. Farsari, and Baron von Stillfried, among others—who set up studios in the treaty ports were relatively uninterested in documenting the dramatic transformation of Japanese society taking place around them. Their chief concern seems to have been to record images of the traditional Japanese culture that was fast disappearing rather than to send back to Europe pictures of Victorian buildings in Tokyo, railroads, or Japanese ladies in bustles and evening gowns. After all, plenty of good pictures of Western life could be gotten on the streets of Europe or America; why waste energy and film on capturing less attractive versions in Japan? Far more intriguing for them were the exotic features of this strange land that was still so different from the countries of the West. Their pictures of samurai in full battle regalia, or court ladies in aristocratic Heian-period costume, or actors frozen in scenes from the kabuki theatre are self-conscious attempts to preserve or re-create the pre-Meiji Japanese past. Inspiring the foreign photographers and their Japanese disciples must have been an awareness that what remained "purely Japanese" in the cultural manifestations of the period was destined for rapid extinction. The archaic figures illustrated in Ogawa's albums *Japanese Costume Before the Restoration* and *Military Costume of Old Japan* were captured on film to preserve for future generations imagery from the Japanese past that could still be reassembled but might any day disappear before the onslaught of modernization.

But whether inspired by a zeal to document, a seeking for exotica, or an impulse to preserve historical images, the products of the Meiji photographers offer us an endlessly fascinating view of Japan at one of the most dramatic moments in her long history. Gazing out at us from the pictures are Japanese individuals who, while sitting in the photographer's studio, might have been confident or apprehensive about the current affairs of their society, bewildered by the whirlwind changes in their lives or secure in their positivist conviction that their lot was improving. Whatever their mental state, they silently tell us much through their appearance and their gestures about what life was like in the years of Meiji.

Peter Grilli

FELIX BEATO   *Mt. Fuji from Yokohama,* 1867.
Albumen Print, 28.9 x 20.6 cm.

13

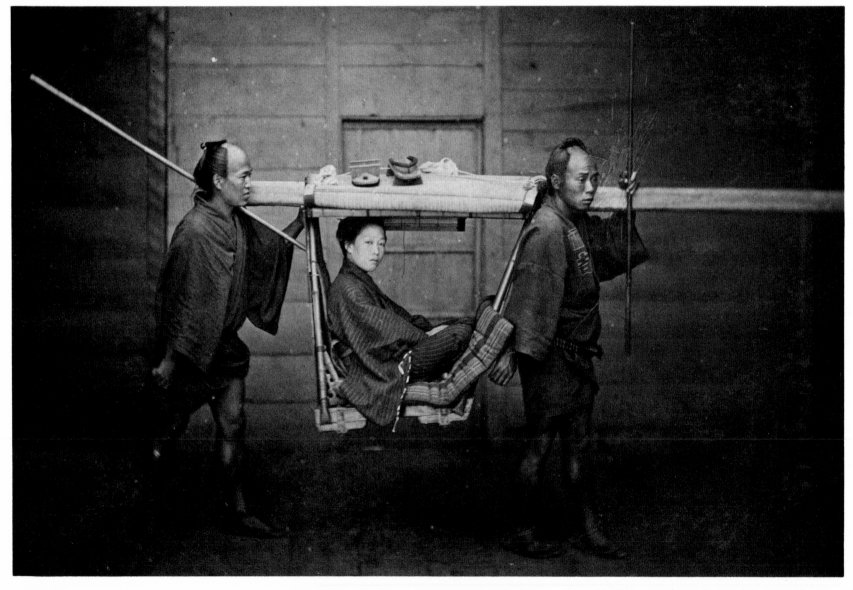

FELIX BEATO *Woman in Kago*, 1864–65.
In the highest classes of Japanese society kago bearers were selected for their symmetry of shape and muscular development. They were treated with as much care as a European sovereign gave to the training of his most elegant thoroughbreds. Albumen Print, 19 x 13 cm.

OGAWA ISSHIN   *A Knight of the Kamakura Period*
(from Military Costume in Old Japan), 1890.
During the Kamakura period (1185–1336) the bow was
used extensively; the bag-like appendage on the
samurai's back (horo) spread out during a charge to
ward off enemy arrows. Albumen Print, 21.5 x 26 cm.

16

FELIX BEATO   *Woman in Winter Costume,* 1867–68.
Albumen Print, 23 x 28.9 cm.

FELIX BEATO *Woman at Toilet*, 1867–68.
In traditional Japan a white neck was regarded as a mark of great beauty; lips were painted red with
vegetable dye (violet if the dye was applied more thickly). Until the 1870s, it was fashionable for
Japanese married women to blacken their teeth. Albumen Print, 25.5 x 20.3 cm.

A. FARSARI & CO. *Mogi Road,* 1890s.
Albumen Print, 25.3 x 20 cm.

FELIX BEATO *Boat in Front of Village,* 1867–68.
Albumen Print, 29.5 x 26 cm.

19

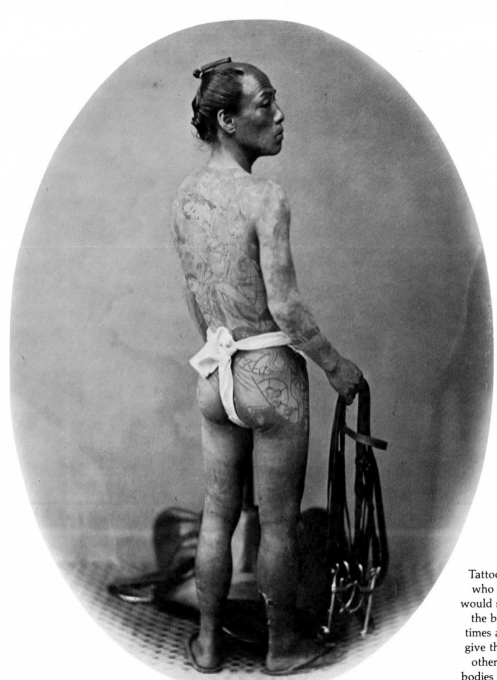

FELIX BEATO *Betto* (Groom), 1867–68.
Tattooing in Japan may have begun with fishermen
who believed that tattoos of demons and dragons
would scare off sharks, or it may have originated with
the branding of criminals. Swashbucklers of feudal
times adorned themselves with scenes of adventure to
give themselves a more terrifying air, and, ultimately,
other classes whose vocations required baring their
bodies in public followed suit, i.e., carpenters and bet-
toes. Albumen Print, 20.7 x 26 cm.

KUSAKABE KIMBEI   *Geisha with Obi Turned Backwards, Ready for Bedding Down,* 1890s. Albumen Print, 29.3 x 24 cm.

KUSAKABE KIMBEI *Buddhist Procession*, 1880s.
Albumen Print, 23.8 x 19 cm.

A. FARSARI & CO. *Futawarasan Shrine at Nikko.*
1890s. Albumen Print, 20.5 x 19.7 cm,

KUSAKABE KIMBEI *Hakone Lake*, 1880s.
Albumen Print, 20.5 x 19.7 cm.

Japan During the Tokugawa Period

Throughout Japan's feudal period (1192–1868), it was the shogun (literally, 'barbarian quelling generalissimo') who exercised real power in the country, while the Emperor was reduced to the status of a puppet, holding sway only in his shadow court at Kyoto. In 1603, Tokugawa Ieyasu obtained the title of shogun and for the next 264 years, the Tokugawa dynasty asserted its dominance over every aspect of Japanese life—personal and governmental. Under their rule, the country retreated into isolation from the rest of the world. A series of prohibitions insured the effectiveness of this decision: Anyone venturing abroad was not allowed to return; the manufacture of large ocean-going ships was forbidden; Christianity was proscribed; Japanese converts (by the Spanish and Portuguese) were mercilessly slaughtered; draconian laws governed the teaching of Confucianism and severe limitations harnessed the press. Through a series of interlocking responsibilities, an individual could not countermand the feudal order without involving others in his crime. Thus, the head of a family was responsible for the family unit, the village headman accounted for the misdeeds of the townspeople, and finally, the daimyo (feudal lord) bore the burden for the actions of his clan. The entire group would be punished for a crime committed by one of its members.

During the Tokugawa reign, there were approximately 1,500 peasant revolts against the strict hieratic structure of Japanese society which provided no legal recourse for individual injustice. In the rigid division of social classes samurai led by the daimyo sat atop the feudal structure, followed by peasants, artisans, and tradesmen, who, motivated strictly by profit, were considered a degraded class.

FELIX BEATO *The Tokaido*, 1867–68.
The great highway linking the eastern Kanto region with the Kyoto-Osaka area in the west, the Tokaido was one of the five main roads of Japan used by the feudal lords (daimyo) to travel to Edo (present-day Tokyo). During the Tokugawa period, most daimyo were forced to spend semiannual periods in Edo in attendance on the shogun. When they returned to their provincial domains, they were required to leave their wives and families in Edo as hostages of the shogun. Albumen Print, 27.8 x 23 cm.

FELIX BEATO *View of Hakone Village,* 1867–68.
At each village entrance was a barrier gate (sekisho)
through which all passersby had to move, removing
their hats for inspection by the local guard. Albumen
Print, 28.8 x 22 cm.

FELIX BEATO *Nagasaki*, 1867–68.
Nagasaki, a seaport on the western coast of Kyushu,
was the single window to the outside world during the
seclusionist rule of the Tokugawa shogunate. After
Japan was officially closed in 1636, a few Chinese and
Dutch merchants were permitted to continue their
commercial activities under rigid shogunate controls.
Albumen Print, 29 x 22 cm.

HERBERT POINTING *On Top of Mt. Fuji,* 1901–6.
Gelatine Bromide Print, 16.5 x 12 cm.

PHOTOGRAPHER UNKNOWN *Nishimashi Village*, 1870s.
Albumen Print, 20 x 15.5 cm.

In the country of the gods, he who lifts his hand
against his parents, or against the elders of his family,
against his master or his teacher is reckoned guilty of
a foul and heinous crime, and is condemned to die by
spears upon the cross. — 1868 Caption.

FELIX BEATO *The Execution Ground*, 1867–68.
The crucified prisoner is Sokichi, aged 23, a servant
guilty of killing Nikisasuro, son of his master Nuiske
at the village of Kiso. Albumen Print, 28.5 x 22.2 cm.

FELIX BEATO *Giant Buddha at Kamakura, 1867–68.*
Albumen Print, 26.2 x 20.9 cm.

33

KUSAKABE KIMBEI *Samurai Bowman*, 1880s.
Albumen Print, 21.5 x 27.3 cm.

FELIX BEATO *Ford at Sakana-Nagawa.* 1866–67.
Albumen Print, 29 x 22 cm.

FELIX BEATO *Samurai in Armor*, 1867.
Koboto Santaro [sic], commander-in-chief of the
shogun's army, who was killed while resisting the pro-
restoration forces. Albumen Print, 22.5 x 29 cm.

The Meiji Restoration

During the decade of the 1860s, the Emperor's court at Kyoto became the center for anti-Tokugawa dissidents who disagreed with the traditionalist, conservative policies of the shogunate. In 1868, legitimist forces occupied the city of Edo (subsequently renamed Tokyo or "eastern capital"), restoring to power a fourteen-year-old boy who became the Emperor Meiji. The irony of the Meiji restoration was that the most traditional form of monarchy was endorsed by progressives seeking to modernize Japan by bringing to an end the feudal period of the shoguns.

Waves of reform followed the Emperor Meiji's assumption of power: the shogun and feudal samurai were stripped of their power; Tokyo became the seat of a centralized government and hundreds of European advisors were imported to help Japan modernize. New role models were selected—Britain for a modern navy, France for an army, and Germany for a general staff. Although the progressives' proclaimed goal was to modernize not Westernize, it became apparent that the two were interchangeable when government officials took up the waltz and quadrille as emblems of modernity. In the early 1870s, a government edict instructed samurai to shave their top knots and to desist from wearing swords. As railways and shipyards were built, an even stronger impetus was given to incoming Western influence. The Emperor himself was persuaded to eat beef in order to convince the populace that the Buddhist injunction against animal flesh was not only unhealthy but unprogressive as well.

FELIX BEATO   *Samurai Outside the Palace of the Daimyo of Satsuma, Edo* [Tokyo], 1867.
On January 19, 1868, the palace was burned and several hundred Satsuma samurai, along with their wives and children, were massacred. This was one in a chain of events leading to the overthrow of the Tokugawa shogunate by a coalition of forces from Satsuma, Choshu, and other anti-Tokugawa domains. Albumen Print, 29 x 21.8 cm.

38

UCHIDA KYUICHI   *Haru-ko, the Empress of Japan,*
1872.   Albumen Print, 19.7 x 26.4 cm.

UCHIDA KYUICHI *Mutsuhito, the Emperor Meiji*, 1872.
Prince Mutsuhito became Emperor in January 1867, at
the age of fourteen, and his reign lasted forty-five
years. In 1868, his reign-period was given the auspi-
cious title Meiji (lit., 'Enlightened Rule'), and he
became the personal symbol of the entire modernization of Japan. Emperor Meiji is traditionally considered the one hundred twenty-second ruler in a
dynasty that traces its theoretical origin to the
mythological first Emperor Jimmu Tenno, who took
the throne in 660 B.C. Meiji's grandson Hirohito is the
present Emperor, whose reign-period is known as
Showa (lit., 'Brilliant Peace'). Albumen Print,
21 x 25.2 cm.

OGAWA ISSHIN *A Female Warrior of the Kamakura Period (from* Military Costume in Old Japan*),* 1890. The Kamakura period (1185–1333) was a time of civil war and intense military activity. Although warfare was not ordinarily the pursuit of women, several wives of great generals are known to have followed their husbands into battle. Albumen Print, 27.2 x 21 cm.

OGAWA ISSHIN   *Foot Soldier (from* Military Costume in Old Japan*),* 1890.
An armed retainer of the Fujiwara period (860-1160) wearing light armor;
the weapon is the naginata.   Albumen Print, 21.5 x 26.5 cm.   **43**

OGAWA ISSHIN *A Fighting Monk of the Kamakura Period (from* Military Costume in Old Japan), 1890. From about the eleventh century on, Buddhist monasteries maintained corps of belligerent monks; this Buddhist soldier wears clerical robes over his armor and his head is covered by the sacred kesa (head cowl). Albumen Print, 20.8 x 25.6 cm.

44

OGAWA ISSHIN *A Warrior of the Nambokucho Period (from* Military Costume in Old Japan*)*, 1890.
This armor was in use during the Wars of Succession between the northern and southern dynasties (1336–92). The distinctive parts of the armor are throat-cover, knee-cover, sleeve badges, and the helmet badge used to distinguish friend from foe. Albumen Print, 21 x 26 cm.

BARON VON STILLFRIED *Waiter and Customer*, 1870s.
Albumen Print, 19.5 x 23.8 cm.

The Modernization of Japan

The following notes were made in 1904 by Basil Hall Chamberlain, the foremost cultural anthologist of the passing Japanese scene. They reflect a Victorian view of the modernization of Japan, with a surprising candor about Western interference and Japanese endurance.

History has never witnessed a more sudden *volte-face* [than the restoration of the Emperor and the subsequent plan to modernize Japan]. ...We foreigners, being mere lookers-on, may no doubt sometimes regret the substitution of commonplace European ways for the glitter, the glamour of picturesque Orientalism.... Does not the whole experience of the last three hundred years go to prove that no Oriental state which retains distinctively Oriental institutions can hope to keep its territory free from Western aggression? What of India? What even of China?...From the moment the intelligent Samurai realized that the Europeanization of the country was a question of life and death, they have never ceased carrying on the work of reform and progress.

A centralized bureaucracy was set up, Buddhism was disestablished, an Imperial mint opened, and posts and telegraphs and railways were introduced....At the same time photography, meat eating, and other "Europeanisms" came pell-mell into vogue without official encouragement....1885–87 were the years of the great "foreign fever," when Japanese society was literally submerged in a flood of European athletics, card-playing, foreign dress for ladies, and dancing.

[But] the cloud of discontent that has darkened industrialism in the West already begins to obscure the Japanese sky. The "rights of labour" are asserting themselves. We hear of frequent strikes....Nothing can be imagined further from the whole mental attitude of the working class of even seventeen years ago. For them, as for subjects generally, the watchword was, not rights, but duties.

—Basil Hall Chamberlain, *Things Japanese*

FELIX BEATO *Hachiman Shrine, Kamakura*, 1867–68.
The shrine was built in 1191 by Minamoto Yoritomo,
the great warlord and founder of the Kamakura
shogunate, and was dedicated to the Shinto deity
Hachiman, from whom Yoritomo traced his ancestry.
Albumen Print, 28.5 x 23.5 cm.

KUSAKABE KIMBEI *Benten-dori, Yokohama,* no date.
Albumen Print, 27 x 21 cm.

The origin of the jinrikisha is shrouded in obscurity.
The usual foreign version is that an American named
Goble suggested the idea of a modified perambulator
somewhere about 1867. There are now in 1904 over
33,000 jinrikishas in Tokyo alone....
　　　　—Basil Hall Chamberlain, *Things Japanese*

KUSAKABE KIMBEI　*Jinrikisha Men and Geisha*, 1890s.
Albumen Print, 27.5 x 21 cm.

Japan has been called "a paradise of babies." The babies are generally so good as to help to make it a paradise for adults. The late Mrs. Chaplin-Ayrton tried to explain the goodness of Japanese children by a reference to the furnitureless conditions of Japanese houses. There is nothing, she said, for them to break, nothing for them to be told not to touch.
—Basil Hall Chamberlain, *Things Japanese*

BARON VON STILLFRIED   *Japanese Children, Yokohama,*
1870s. Albumen Print, 19.5 x 24.8 cm.

52

BARON VON STILLFRIED   *Hodo Waterfall, Nikko*, 1870s.
Albumen Print, 20.6 x 26.5 cm.

NAGOYA. 184.

BARON VON STILLFRIED   *Nagoya Castle*, 1870s.
Albumen Print, 21.6 x 27.5 cm.

FELIX BEATO *San-ju-san-gen-do, Kyoto, 1867–68.*
Albumen Print, 28.5 x 22.3 cm.

FELIX BEATO   *Hachiman Shrine, Kamakura, 1867–68.*
Albumen Print, 19.5 x 24 cm.

The first impression made on any fairly observant person landing in Japan is the extraordinary variety of the vegetation....The number of known species of trees and plants (exclusive of mosses, etc.) attains the enormous figure of 2,728 distributed over 941 genera.

—Basil Hall Chamberlain, *Things Japanese*

FELIX BEATO *Miyanoshita*, 1867–68.
Nestled in the Hakone mountains, the village of Miyanoshita was known for its baths. Albumen Print, 31.1 x 24.3 cm.

KUSAKABE KIMBEI *Boat with Village in Background,*
1880s. Albumen Print, 26 x 20 cm.

64

KUSAKABE KIMBEI *Professional Singer,* 1880s.
Albumen Print, 20.5 x 26.7 cm.

KUSAKABE KIMBEI *Rear View of Japanese Woman,*
1880s. Albumen Print, 21 x 27.4 cm.

KUSAKABE KIMBEI *Children*, 1880s.
Albumen Print, 27.6 x 21.4 cm.

KUSAKABE KIMBEI *Prostitute and Attendant*, 1880s.
Albumen Print, 20.6 x 26.8 cm.

95. Moonlight on Hakone, Japan's most beautiful lake.
Copyright 1902 by C. H. Graves.

PHOTOGRAPHER UNKNOWN   *Moonlight on Lake Hakone,* 1902.
Gelatine Bromide Print, 7.8 x 8 cm.

PHOTOGRAPHER UNKNOWN   *Mt. Fuji from Lake
Motosu*, 1904.
Gelatine Bromide Print, 7.8 x 8 cm.

H. C. WHITE   *Tea Harvesting, Ashikubo*, 1907.
Gelatine Bromide Print, 7.8 x 8 cm.

PHOTOGRAPHER UNKNOWN   *Professional Sumo*
Wrestlers, 1905.
Gelatine Bromide Print, 7.8 x 8 cm.

PHOTOGRAPHER UNKNOWN   *Putting on Armor*, 1870s.
Albumen Print, 17.8 x 13.5 cm.

PHOTOGRAPHER UNKNOWN *The Toilet*, 1870s.
Albumen Print, 18 x 13.5 cm.

KUSAKABE KIMBEI *Geisha*, 1890s.
Albumen Print, 19.5 x 24 cm.

74

KUSAKABE KIMBEI *Basket Seller*, 1890s.
Albumen Print, 27.5 x 21 cm.

76

BARON VON STILLFRIED   *Dancer*, 1870s.
Albumen Print, 19.3 x 24 cm.

FELIX BEATO   *Doctor and Patient*, 1867–68.
Japanese society doctors were permitted to wear the
two swords of a samurai rank. Albumen Print, 27.5 x 22.8 cm.

77

KUSAKABE KIMBEI *Itinerant Priests*, 1880s.
Albumen Print, 21 x 27 cm.

KUSAKABE KIMBEI *Prince Hotta's Garden at Tokyo,*
1890s. Albumen Print, 25.5 x 19.5 cm.

KUSAKABE KIMBEI *Woman Washing Hair*, 1880s.
Albumen Print, 21 x 27 cm.

HERBERT POINTING   *Mt. Fuji*, 1901–6.
Gelatine Bromide Print, 12 x 16.5 cm.

Felix Beato

FELIX BEATO *Samurai, Yokohama, 1864–65.*
Albumen Print, 14.6 x 17.8 cm.

Beato was originally a war photographer who settled in Japan during the 1863–64 period. As the first great European photographer of that country, Beato made extensive documentation of the last years of the medieval period (1865–68). He initiated the practices of hand-coloring photographs and of compiling albums of Japanese types. Beyond his own artistic achievement, Beato had a farreaching influence on all subsequent photography in Japan.

FELIX BEATO   *The Fire Brigade, Yokohama, 1867–68.*
Albumen Print, 24 x 25 cm.

83

84

FELIX BEATO *The Sake Seller,* 1867–68.
Albumen Print, 20.4 x 25.4 cm.

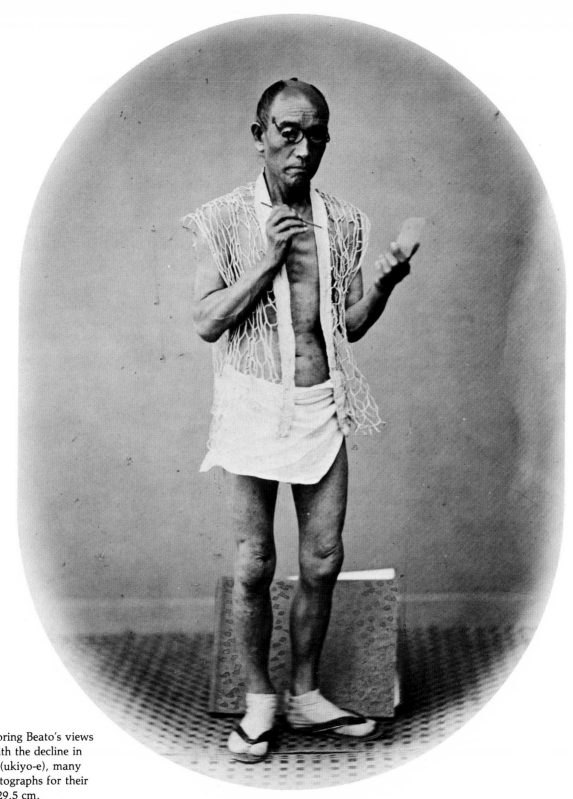

FELIX BEATO *My Artist*, 1867–68.
The artist responsible for hand-coloring Beato's views
of Japan holds a carte-de-visite. With the decline in
popularity of the woodblock print (ukiyo-e), many
artists turned to hand coloring photographs for their
livelihood. Albumen Print, 21.6 x 29.5 cm.

FELIX BEATO *View of the Tokaido*, 1867–68.
Albumen Print, 27.6 x 23.7 cm.

FELIX BEATO *The Canal and Market, Gankiro*, 1864–65.
One of the few surviving views of Yokohama before it
was destroyed by fire on November 26, 1866.
Albumen Print, 30 x 21.7 cm.

FELIX BEATO *Nagasaki*, 1864–65.
Albumen Print, 28 x 21 cm.

FELIX BEATO   *Rokubu*, 1867–68.
The rokubu was an itinerant priest of the Buddhist
sect of Ko-sodate-jizo. He was summoned to restore
barren women to fertility and carried on his back a
portable altar equipped with his religious parapher-
nalia. He was supported solely by charitable contribu-
tions. Albumen Print, 22.5 x 29 cm.

FELIX BEATO   *Laborer*, 1867–68.
Albumen Print, 23.6 x 28.3 cm.

A. Le Bas

An amateur photographer, Le Bas was most likely a French naval officer who accompanied the Shimonoseki Expedition (1864) that captured the forts of the Choshu clan. Le Bas specialized in photographs that were so elaborately retouched on the plate it is difficult not to call his work photographic drawings.

A. LE BAS   *Hachiman Shrine, Shimonoseki,* 1864.
Albumen Print, 16.2 x 12 cm.

A. LE BAS *Samurai, Choshu*, 1864.
In 1864, a fleet of British, French, Dutch, and
American ships attacked the forts of the Satsuma clan
at Shimonoseki, thereby reopening the straits to European vessels. Albumen Print, 16.5 x 12.5 cm.

94

A. LE BAS *Samurai in Armor*, 1864.
Albumen Print, 12.5 x 16.5 cm.

A. LE BAS *Samurai in Armor,* 1864.
Albumen Print, 12.5 x 16.5 cm.

Baron von Stillfried

One of the great photographers of the Japanese scene, Baron von Stillfried bought Beato's studio (1877) and continued to develop the genre of the closely observed studio portrait. His work is characterized by a remorseless psychological intensity that is heightened by blank studio backdrops and a minimum of props.

BARON VON STILLFRIED   *Woman*, 1870s.
Albumen Print, 19.5 x 24.2 cm.

BARON VON STILLFRIED   *Samurai*, 1870s.
Albumen Print, 19.3 x 24.2 cm.

BARON VON STILLFRIED *Woman with Umbrella,* 1870s.
Wires attached to the clothing create the effect of
wind and streaks scratched in the negative give the
illusion of rain. Albumen Print, 21.5 x 28 cm.

BARON VON STILLFRIED *Man in Winter Costume*,
1870s. Albumen Print, 21 x 26.5 cm.

313. WRESTLERS

BARON VON STILLFRIED   *Wrestlers*, 1870s.
Albumen Prints, 20 x 23.5 cm.

BARON VON STILLFRIED   *Sleeping Woman*, 1870s.
Albumen Print, 20 x 23.5 cm.

BARON VON STILLFRIED *Hair Dressing,* 1870s.
Albumen Print, 19.4 x 25.4 cm.

BARON VON STILLFRIED *Women*, 1870s.
Albumen Prints, 10.5 x 14 cm.

BARON VON STILLFRIED *Child Acrobats*, 1870s.
Albumen Print, 17.7 x 25.7 cm.

Kusakabe Kimbei

Kusakabe was the great Japanese commercial photographer of the nineteenth century. There is a direct causal link between the work of Beato, Stillfried, and Kusakabe which is the culmination of a cross-cultural view of Japan during the period. It is probable that Kusakabe began as Stillfried's operator, eventually buying his stock when the latter departed from Japan in the mid-1880s. He operated his own firm until 1912, when he disappeared from view. Kusakabe's specialty was the penetrating studio portrait of the Japanese sitter.

KUSAKABE KIMBEI *Shinto Pilgrim*, 1880s.
Albumen Print, 20.5 x 27.5 cm.

KUSAKABE KIMBEI *Actors*, 1880s.
Albumen Print, 27 x 21.2 cm.

KUSAKABE KIMBEI *Geisha*, 1880s.
Albumen Print, 20.5 x 21.2 cm.

108

KUSAKABE KIMBEI   *Geisha*, 1880s.
Albumen Print, 20.7 x 27.3 cm.

110

KUSAKABE KIMBEI   *Vegetable Vendor,* 1880s.
Albumen Print, 26.8 x 21 cm.

765. BELL. NIKKO

KUSAKABE KIMBEI *Bell, Nikko*, 1890s.
Albumen Print, 26 x 19.7 cm.

KUSAKABE KIMBEI *Workmen's Holiday*, 1890s.
Albumen Print, 20 x 23.5 cm.

KUSAKABE KIMBEI   *Vendor of Pickled Vegetables,*
1880s. Albumen Print, 26.8 x 21 cm.

114

KUSAKABE KIMBEI   *Child Acrobats*, 1880s.
Albumen Print, 28 x 21 cm.

Ogawa Isshin

The most successful society photographer of nineteenth-century Japan, Ogawa's work must be considered in the context of a renaissance of traditional Japanese art during the period 1880–90, which sought to reveal profound spiritual values through a careful study of Japanese cultural forms.

OGAWA ISSHIN *A Young Warrior (from* Military Costume in Old Japan), 1890.   This is a particular illustration of a Kamakura period (1185–1336) young samurai affecting effeminate manners and personal decoration. Collotype, 21.9 x 21.5 cm.

OGAWA ISSHIN *Court Lady of the Fujiwara Period*
(*from* Japanese Costume Before the Restoration), 1890.
During the Fujiwara period (866-1160), women of the
court wore twelve-layered robes of silk brocade with
wide sleeves and a long train. This type of costume is
still worn for imperial weddings or coronations.
Albumen Print, 21 x 25 cm.

OGAWA ISSHIN *Classical Actor*, 1890.
Albumen Print, 21.5 x 26 cm.

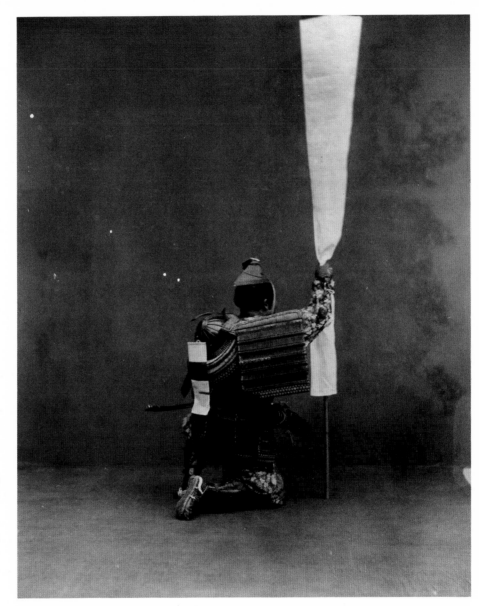

OGAWA ISSHIN   *Flag Bearer (from* Military Costume in Old Japan*)*, 1890.
During the Nambukucho period (1336–1392), flag bearers were chosen from good families. This samurai wears the badge of the Nitta clan (descended from Minamoto Yoshisige); a whip is stuck in his belt and he wears a backplate (seita) which was part of the light armor worn during the period.
Albumen Print, 27 x 19.1 cm.

119

OGAWA ISSHIN   *Hakuwo Lily (from* Lilies of Japan*)*,
1890. Collotype, 13.5 x 22.5 cm.

OGAWA ISSHIN   *Tametomo Lily (from* Lilies of Japan*),*
1890. Collotype, 21.5 x 26 cm.

121

OGAWA ISSHIN   *The Discovery of Morono (Kira),*
(from The Forty Seven Ronin), 1890.
A key episode from the Japanese classic on samurai
life. Collotype, 26 x 20 cm.

OGAWA ISSHIN *Lady Enya Recognizes Nitta's Helmet*
(from The Forty Seven Ronin*)*, 1890.
Collotype, 27 x 21.9 cm.

123

Tamamura K.

Tamamura was a competitor of Kusakabe Kimbei in Yokohama and worked during the period 1890–1910. Throughout the 1890s Tamamura specialized in hand-tinted views of Japanese scenes and native types. As late as 1915 the firm of Tamamura was still in business in Yokohama.

TAMAMURA K.   *Two Samurai, Yokohama*, 1890s.
Albumen Print, 9.3 x 13.4 cm.

124

TAMAMURA K. *Two Geisha, Yokohama, 1890s.*
Albumen Print, 9.3 x 13 cm.

TAMAMURA K.   *Woman with Flowers,*
Yokohama, 1890s.
Albumen Print, 9.3 x 13.5 cm.

126

TAMAMURA K. *Collage of Baby Pictures,*
Yokohama, 1890s.
Albumen Print, 9.5 x 13.3 cm.

Photography in Nineteenth-Century Japan

The tradition of topographical photography begins with the invention of the camera, for no sooner had this tool become available than adventurous travelers realized its possibilities. Photographs of the pyramids were taken just a few months after the daguerreotype process was published in Paris; intrepid photographers reached the heights of the Himalayan mountains, the remote jungles of Burma, and the inaccessible countries of the Orient, armed with the same resolve to discover unknown terrain and capture it on film. In some countries, photography became firmly rooted as an art form. Usually beginning as a tourist commodity, it often grew into a popular industry in its own right. In India and China, however, where imperialist Western influence extended clearly into the photographic domain, an indigenous, recognizable style of native photography either did not develop or was overshadowed by the desire to imitate Western approaches to the new "art-science."[1]

In contrast, photography in Japan retained a distinct Japanese style with unique characteristics. Perhaps the existence of an already popular tradition of woodblock prints (ukiyo-e) and paper stencils (kata-gami) enabled the Japanese to adapt photographic conventions to something familiar in their own culture. Perhaps their age-old fascination with paper itself or their incredible facility with craft-making accounts for some of the enthusiasm which was subsequently evidenced in their photography. Perhaps it was simply that the Japanese culture, unlike the Indian and Chinese, had not been adulterated by Western influences during the nineteenth century and therefore had maintained a strong sense of its own identity intact. Whatever the reason, there is no doubt that the greatest reciprocity of cross-cultural influence in the Far Asian photography of that period occurred in Japan.

Although there were hundreds of photographers working in nineteenth-century Japan—many of whom remain anonymous—the development of a Japanese vision in photography can be attributed to a heterogeneous mix of talents, among whom were an Italian military photographer (Felix Beato), an Austrian nobleman (Baron von Stillfried), a Japanese photographer of tourist views (Kusakabe Kimbei), and the most successful Japanese society photographer of the period (Ogawa Isshin). The interval covered by their work dates from the early 1860s to the first decade of the twentieth century, a period of time which coincides with Japan's transformation from an insular, feudal country to a modern world power.

Of interest to any study of photography during this period is a description of the political background against which both European and Japanese photographers had to work. For two centuries (1630-1854), Japan had been a country that was closed to foreigners. The sole exceptions to this self-imposed quarantine from the rest of the world were two tiny trading enclaves maintained by Chinese and Dutch merchants. The Japanese government of the Tokugawa shoguns allowed eleven Dutchmen to reside in Japan at the Dutch factory on Deshima, a small island opposite Nagasaki, approximately 600 feet long by 240 feet wide. This settlement was a minuscule window through which the Japanese could peer at the remote events of Europe and take from Europe, in a highly selective way, those few things it wanted. It was through this seemingly inconsequential opening to the West that the rudiments of European mathematics, geography, medicine, and, perhaps, even the first camera were introduced into Japan.

In 1854, the Japanese government of the shogun was forced by an American diplomatic ultimatum, presented by Commodore Matthew C. Perry, to "open" the country to the West. With this forced access, Westerners discovered a society that was traditional, insular, and at times homicidally xenophobic, ruled by a government that had steadfastly refused to acknowledge the existence of the outside world for more than two centuries. Yet within four decades, Japan had emerged from this isolation to become an industrial power capable of waging war against Russia (the largest of the European nation-states)—routing its armies, defeating its admirals, and sinking two of its three fleets. A score of Japanese and European photographers were on hand documenting the outcome of the Russo-Japanese War to an in-credulous world. But just as the camera recorded dramatic military and political confrontations, it also witnessed the subtler changes accompanying the decline of a traditional Asian culture, for in a sense medieval Japan was like an oyster—to open it was to kill it.

Perhaps not surprisingly, it was through the particular conceit of the American government that Commodore Perry on his diplomatic mission was accompanied by a daguerreotypist, Acting Master's Mate Eliphalet Brown, Jr. From February 7, 1854, when Perry's squadron returned to Japan to hear the result of the ultimatum delivered the previous summer, to June 28, 1854, when they sailed away after the conclusion of a treaty, Brown made a series of daguerreotypes which were the first datable photographs done in Japan. Officially sanctioned, this work documented village and town scenes, a variety of Japanese types and the personae of the Japanese-American diplomatic gatherings. Upon the return of the expedition, these daguerreotypes were used as models for wood engravings and lithographic plates published in the official report of the expedition by Francis Hawks.[2] Unfortunately, in the course of producing the plates for this work, the Philadelphia lithographic establishment which undertook the printing burned down and Brown's daguerreotypes were destroyed. As a small solace the engravings and lithographs remain to give some indication of what Japan was like at the time of the Perry expedition.[3]

Commercial Photography in Japan

The invention of the camera provided the West with its first look at what Asia was really like. To satisfy this curiosity both European and Japanese photographers created commercial views of scenery and local types which were sold to tourists, much as today's souvenir postcards and slides are. These photographs were the professional productions of a highly competitive field and became immensely popular during the latter part of the nineteenth century. In addition to their use as mementoes, commercial albums served as decorative travelogues for people who were fascinated by the Orient but unable to travel there themselves.

Thus the best documentation of the last years of Tokugawa Japan to the beginning of the modern era (the Meiji period) was made by commercial photographers who created their "views" for the export market. Commercial photography of the scenes and types apparently enjoyed little local patronage in Far Asian countries. Consequently, an entire genre, developed first by European photographers, then further adapted by Japanese photographers, was preserved by its popularity outside of the country whose life it captured.

European Commercial Photography

Photography attained widespread popularity in Europe during the 1840s, but there was no extensive professional activity in Japan until the 1860s. Though Japan had been "opened" in 1854, it actually took years of delicate negotiation with the government of the shogun to set up the treaty ports of Nagasaki and Yokohama where foreigners were allowed to reside and trade. The earliest European settlers in those treaty ports were usually more intent on making quick fortunes than in discovering the hidden mysteries of the interior of Japan or practicing the "art-science" of photography. By the 1860s, drastic political changes had shattered the social structure of medieval Japan and with it, the government of the Tokugawa shoguns. These changes ultimately resulted in the restoration of the Emperor to the center of Japanese political life. Up to that time, Japanese politics, to the European resident in the country, were lethally divided between two factions—the conservative (anti-foreign) and the progressive (pro-foreign).

Conservative samurai adopted assassination as their method of protest against progressive Japanese politicians and Europeans. In 1859, the year the treaty ports were opened, five Europeans were killed. Two years later, the secretary of the American Legation, Henry Heusken, was killed. Then, on the night of July 5, 1861, twenty-eight samurai attempted, in a single attack, to assassinate the entire British diplomatic corps in Tokyo (Edo, as it was then called). Among the survivors of the attack were Gower, a secretary of the mission, and Charles Wirgman, a free-lance artist for the *London Illustrated News.* Wirgman was at the British Legation that night to join Sir Rutherford Alcock, the British minister to Japan, on his intended overland trip from Nagasaki to Tokyo, which was, as Alcock noted in his journal, "an opportunity never likely to return."[4] A description of how Wirgman fared that night was offered by Laurence Oliphant, himself severely slashed by a samurai.

About this time, Mr. Wirgman, the artist of the *Illustrated News* turned up, coated with a thick breast plate of mud. He had taken refuge under the house, which was raised about eighteen inches from the ground, and, crawling in on his stomach, had remained in profound but somewhat dirty security under the flooring.[5]

What Oliphant did not realize was that Wirgman, in selecting his hideout, was nearly killed by Consul Morrison, when the latter, standing directly above Wirgman's head, emptied his revolver first into the floor, and then, with better aim, into his and Oliphant's attackers.

In late 1861, Gower brought out the first commercially produced photographs of Japan. Entitled "Views of Japan," they were published by the firm of Negretti & Zambra in London. Although the series caused a sensation, Gower strangely disappeared from the photographic scene.[6]

Charles Wirgman became one of the central figures of the European community in Japan for the next thirty years and was instrumental in bringing to that country one of the greatest European photographers of the nineteenth century, Felix Beato.

Wirgman first met Beato when both men covered the Anglo-French military expedition that succeeded in occupying Imperial Peking (and burning the Summer Palace complex) in late 1860. From China, Wirgman had continued on to Japan, while Beato had gone to the Levant and to Egypt. Although the first mention of Beato in Japan is in mid-1864, when he served as official photographer of the Shimonoseki Expedition,[7] it was probably through his friendship with Wirgman that Beato was tempted to travel to Japan and begin work there.

In 1865, the firm of Beato & Wirgman, Artists & Photographers, was founded, and it continued to operate successfully until 1869. From 1869 to 1877 Beato operated his own studio, F. Beato & Co., Photographers. In 1877, Beato sold his studio to Baron von Stillfried but remained in Yokohama as a general merchant until 1884.[8] What Beato saw in the Japan of those years, away from the treaty ports, had been virtually unexplored by Europeans, who were prohibited from traveling more than twenty-four miles inland. Japan was as much *terra incognita* as those livid blank spots shaded pink on the map of Africa. Moreover, the hostility to foreigners had become so great that a European never went anywhere unless he was armed with a revolver. Aimé Humbert, the Swiss Envoy to Japan who accompanied Beato to Tokyo was the first to describe the photographer and his work in that country.

> The appearance of our party, which would have occasioned a mob in any densely populated part of Europe did not cause the least sensation....Fingers were only occasionally pointed at our cigars, or at the revolvers in our belts.[9]

Whenever a diplomatic party moved from its legation, it was always accompanied by soldiers of the shogun—this not so much to discourage the movements of Europeans but to protect them. Humbert recounted the following anecdote illustrating the difficulty Beato had in taking views in Tokyo.

> On our right extended the magnificent shade of the park of the Prince of Satsuma...on our left the wall of enclosure of a palace of the Prince of Arima....Mr. Beato set to work to procure a photograph of this peaceful picture when two officers of the prince hastily approached him, and insisted he should desist from the operation. Metman begged them to go first and ascertain the commands of their master....Returning in a few minutes, they declared that the prince absolutely refused to permit that any view whatever of his palace should be taken. Beato bowed respectfully, and ordered the porters to carry away the instrument. The officers withdrew, satisfied, not suspecting that the artist had time to expose two negatives during their brief absence. The guards of our

escort, impassive witnesses of the scene were unanimous in applauding the success of the stratagem.[10]

In 1866, a raging fire devastated Yokohama, and it is probable that most of Beato's (as well as Wirgman's) work was destroyed in the flames. This included his large plate photographs of the opening of China in 1860 and most of the Japanese work done in the pre-1866 period. (It is ironic that the early daguerreotypes done by Eliphalet Brown were also consumed by fire on the other side of the world). Although this loss was irreparable, Beato seemed to redouble his creative efforts and during the next year, he produced a series of sublime scenic views and studio portraits.[11] Within a single year, he sought to replace a stock of negatives that had taken ten years to produce. Although he accomplished this herculean task, the effort seems to have exhausted him creatively. After 1869, Beato's work began to gradually decline until he finally sold out to his competitor, Stillfried, in 1877.

In 1868, Beato began to issue the work which marked the culmination of his photographic career. In two volumes, *Native Types* and *Views of Japan*, it was ponderously titled *Photographic Views of Japan with Historical and Descriptive Notes, Compiled from Authentic Sources, and Personal Observation During a Residence of Several Years (with letterpress by James W. Murray)*. Each volume of the work contained approximately one hundred tipped-in photographs, each mounted opposite a lengthy printed caption. *Views* consisted of full-plate black-and-white albumen photography, while *Native Types* contained elaborately hand-colored albumen prints of Japanese people. Of particular interest in the latter album is "My Artist" (page 85), a

photograph of the Japanese painter responsible for hand-tinting Beato's pictures.

It was undoubtedly Wirgman who influenced Beato to employ Japanese artists to color his prints.[12] Given a long tradition among the Japanese of meticulous hand-painting of paper stencil designs onto fabrics plus their frequent occupation in the decoration of everyday objects, it is not hard to understand why coloring photographs would have such immediate appeal. In Wirgman, Beato had an informant who was not only sensitive to Japanese tradition but also eminently knowledgeable about the conventions of Japanese art, specifically the ukiyo-e (woodblock print). The striking similarities between this art form and Beato's photographs are apparent in the groupings of sitters, the props used, and even in the attitudes and trades of the subjects—blind shampooers, geisha, tradesmen, et cetera. Beato's work was a marked departure from the picturesque and sentimentalized commercial views of the period.

The full measure of Beato's talent can best be seen in his photographs of the Japanese landscape. With the possible exception of the Himalayan photographs of Samuel Bourne (1863–66), the work of no other photographer of the Asian landscape approached the subject as freshly or as delicately. Surprisingly, nowhere in Beato's pre-Japan work was there any indication of his great facility with this genre. It is possible that he was inspired by the Japanese treatment of landscape which is more lyrical and abstract than the European. Few of the great landscapes have survived in pristine condition; by 1871, the negatives already showed signs of severe chipping, and Beato had to spot them radically to make them saleable. Notwithstanding these imperfections, Beato's contribution to the history of photography in Japan was immeasurable. Throughout the decades that followed (1870–1910), virtually every other photographer of the Japanese commercial scene felt obliged to cater to the clientele Beato had first identified. In time, the hand-colored studio photograph of the native type, often carried to garish extremes, became synonymous with Japanese commercial photography and far outlasted its creator.

During the nineteenth century, many photographers from Europe and America visited Japan but few took up residence. In 1865, the *Photographic News* carried a tongue-in-cheek notice concerning commercial photography in Japan in the wake of the first Japanese diplomatic mission to Europe.

> In Japan, it appears, the excitement caused by the *portraits cartes* of the Imperial family (of France) brought back by the Japanese Ambassadors has not subsided. An immense order has reached Paris for photographs of all the European Royalty. This good news has spread like wildfire among despairing photographers and no less than 200 are about to start for that remote region.[13]

The expected boatload of hungry photographers never turned up, but in 1871, the second (and last) great European commercial photographer of Japan appeared in Yokohama.

Baron R. von Stillfried, an Austrian nobleman, first became interested in photographing Asia during the course of his travels in Siam and China. In Japan, he operated a series of studios that seemed to change names with almost seasonal regularity: Stillfried & Co., The Yokohama Library, The Japan Photographic Association, and Stillfried & Andersen (which bought Beato's studio in 1877). In imitation of Beato's work, Stillfried & Andersen produced a photographic album entitled "Views and Costumes of Japan." An unexpected impetus to this work occurred when the Japanese government issued an imperial edict forbidding samurai to wear topknots and to carry swords. Almost dutifully, swarms of samurai trooped off to the photographer's studio to record the way they looked before altering their appearance to become modern. Providentially, the edict gave Stillfried the opportunity to document a variety of Japanese types that overnight disappeared from the scene.

Despite Baron Stillfried's exaggerated claim to have trained "nine-tenths of the Japanese photographers in Japan,"[14] he does deserve credit for having been the first European photographer in the country to make extensive use of Japanese apprentices, among whom was Kusakabe Kimbei, who later developed into the great Japanese talent of the nineteenth century. Kusakabe bought Stillfried's stock in 1885 (when the latter left Japan) and carried on the tradition of the closely observed studio portrait of the Japanese "type." In the work of Beato, Stillfried, and Kusakabe we can see the evolution of an eclectic Japanese view of studio photographs that over the years 1864–90 became the definitive set piece of nineteenth-century photography in Japan.

Beato's studio photographs, which began the genre, are largely documentary with the sitter speaking clearly to the viewer of his situation and social position. Stillfried and Kusakabe produced work more psychological in character, offering insight into the emotional world of the sitter and very often impaling the subject against the backdrop of the studio. Stillfried's scenes were sparingly arranged with few props in evidence; some stones on the ground, perhaps a tea pot or tonsu chest are the only objects that lend versimilitude to his studio photographs. In fact, in his powerful picture of Japanese wrestlers (page 100) no props are used at all, but the stance of the figures and their eccentric composition creates an effect which is totally original. In a pose often found in Japanese prints, the figure at the center stands with his back to the camera; in this case, his nudity further commands attention.

In his photograph of two child acrobats (page 105), Stillfried arrests all sense of movement, heightening the tension of the two figures who are crouched as if ready to spring at the viewer. Purposely removed from their milieu and posed against a blank studio backdrop, Stillfried's subjects become abstract and loom larger than life. Out of context, their expressions and characteristics are ambiguous and slightly menacing. These photographs are not conventional portraits as much as they are fantasies which elicit from the viewer an uneasy shock of recognition.

Stillfried's protege Kusakabe Kimbei must be considered along with the European commercial photographers since he was so directly influenced by their work. Little is known of his career beyond the fact that he was Stillfried's apprentice and ultimately bought his stock. From 1885–1912, Kusakabe operated a commercial studio that catered to tourists in Yokohama; after 1912, his name is no longer listed in any commercial directories nor do any traces of his studio remain. Kusakabe continued in the same tradition as Stillfried but perfected the art of the psychological portrait. In his picture of the geisha (page 109), he presents a view of a woman whose uncompromising stare forces us to consider her apart from the preconceptions one associates with her profession; this geisha is more disturbing than pleasing. The photograph is a superb example of Kusakabe's ability to individualize the conventional photography of "types."

Japanese Commercial Photography

During the 1850s and 1860s in Japan and China, the use of the camera was taboo; to be exposed to its "eye" ensured a sudden or premature death. Photography was always considered a process of the West, but after the initial hostility was overcome, photography was regarded in Japan first with curiosity and then with enthusiasm. As an indication of how culturally acceptable it became, patrons of a Japanese brothel made their selections from still photographs rather than live models.

Shimooka Renjo is credited with being the first Japanese commercial photographer to open a studio.[15] Around 1859, he established himself in the new treaty port of Yokohama and, by 1868, found business so good that he expanded his operations to include a lithographic press and another floor to his studio. In 1893, Shimooka was rewarded for his contribution to the field by his election to the Photographic Society of Japan.

Another noteworthy Japanese photographer of the early period was Uyeno Hikoma, the son of a wealthy Nagasaki merchant, who had been introduced to photographic processes when he attended the first college of chemistry in Japan. In 1860, he bought a camera from a Dutch merchant and took it with him to Tokyo, where he photographed various high ranking officials; these are possibly the first photographs made in the capital. From 1862 through the 1890s, the Uyeno Office of Photography was the most prestigious commercial photographic establishment in Nagasaki. Pierre Loti, the French naval officer who wrote extensively of Japan, described a scene in Uyeno's studio during the 1880s with its clientele of national types.

Two ladies of quality, evidently mother and daughter...are sitting together for a cabinet-sized portrait, with the accessories of Louis XV time...the first great ladies of this country I have seen so near, with their long aristocratic faces, dull, lifeless, almost grey by dint of rice powder, and their mouths painted heart-shaped in vivid carmine....Their fragile bodies, outlandishly graceful in posture, are lost in stiff materials....They make me think, I know not why, of great rare insects...of night moths...

Then we have to let several English sailors pass before us, decked out in their white drill clothes, fresh, fat, and pink like little sugar figures who attitudinise in a sheepish manner round the shafts of the columns. At last it is our turn...and on the negative we are shown we look like a supremely ridiculous little family drawn up in a line by a common photographer at a fair.[16]

By the mid-1860s Japanese commercial photography was apparently thriving with the *Photographic News* (London) reporting that in Osaka alone (population 300,000) there were more than forty Japanese photographers kept busy at their professions. A substantial part of this boom stemmed from the establishment of shajos, or open-air studios that took advantage of long summer days. Usually these were nothing more than studio backdrops, hung against a building or a convenient tree, but the fad became increasingly popular and spread to Nagasaki where Kameya Tokujiro and his daughter Kameya Toyo (the first Japanese woman photographer, only her name and dates survive) set up a successful shajo in competition with Uyeno Hikoma.

During the 1870s there were other photographers of note including Yokoyama Matsusaburo, who was best known for his architectural photographs of Nikko and for his photographic oil paintings, and Uchida Kyuichi, a protege of Uyeno Hikoma, who was the only photographer to be granted a sitting by the Emperor Meiji. It is difficult to appreciate what these photographs meant when they appeared. For the first time in history, it was possible to buy an image of a living deity, and the portraits of the Emperor and Empress (pages 40 and 41) became instant icons of the new age. A year after they were taken (1873) the government forbade their sale and circulation, feeling that they constituted an unseemly commercialization of the Emperor.

The two foremost Japanese photographers of the nineteenth century were Kusakabe Kimbei and Ogawa Isshin (also known as Ogawa Kazuma, and Ogawa Kazunao). While Ogawa was the most successful society photographer of the period and Kimbei merely a lowly commercial photographer, both artists have something in common. Until now, they have been largely forgotten.

If Kimbei labored in obscurity, Ogawa Isshin was the epitome of conspicuous success, ultimately being appointed to the prestigious Imperial Board of Artists. Ogawa was a man of many interests and talents. Essentially, his work can be divided into four areas. In scientific and art photography, Ogawa pioneered documentation of the antique arts of Japan in *Kokka*—then and now the leading magazine of the arts. In publishing, he brought out over thirty volumes of his own and other photographers' work. In commercial photography he operated the most famous studios in Tokyo. And in producing photographic supplies, he was the managing director of the largest film-manufacturing firm in Japan.

Some idea of the contemporary opinion of Ogawa can be gathered from the *Journal of the Photographic Society of India*, which reviewed a group of pictures Ogawa had sent to

Calcutta for an international exhibition, "The collection comprises, first a series of portraits and views...for softness and delicacy *these pictures are absolutely unsurpassable*."[17] Ogawa's masterpieces were a series of historical costume photographs of Japanese types that he published in a variety of books, most notably *Military Costume in Old Japan*, *Japanese Costume Before the Restoration*, and *The Forty Seven Ronin*. Additionally, his studies of flowers in works like *The Lilies of Japan* anticipated work done a decade later in America by the Photo-Secession group.

Ogawa's work must be considered in the larger context of a movement popular in Japan during the 1880s and 1890s. This stressed a renaissance of traditional Japanese cultural values and accounted for a cult of Japonistes developing internationally around men like Lafcadio Hearn, Ernest Fenollosa, and Okakura Kakuzo. The fundamental premise of this group was that a study of Japanese art and culture would unlock profound spiritual values. Towards this end Ogawa created his costume studies of "great moments" in Japanese traditional life. Usually, work of this type, suffused with nationalistic "purity," is sentimental and ridiculous; at its worst, it tends to resemble photography for recruiting posters. But Ogawa was a tasteful photographer, whose work never became didactic. His photographs of samurai types wearing ancient specimens of armor are as beautiful as his images of lilies done for a study of botanical specimens.

Amateur Photography

The dating of the first photograph in Japan is surrounded by considerable debate. A daguerreotype attributed to Lord Shimazu Nariakira—discovered in the Shimazu treasure house at Kagoshima in 1975—seemed to confirm a supposition which Koyasu Masabao presented in *Modern Photography*.

> This discovery validated a long-established theory based on fragmentary records, which held that the first daguerreotype camera was imported into Japan on July 1, 1840 by Uyeno Toshinojo [the father of Uyeno Hikoma], a wealthy merchant chemist living in the city of Nagasaki—just about a year after photography had been invented in France. Uyeno reportedly gave (or sold) the camera to Lord Shimazu, who proceeded to record his image on a silver plate on June 1, 1841.[18]

The flaw in this theory is that the camera would have appeared in Japan—then one of the most remote and inaccessible countries on earth—a mere nine months after the daguerreotype process was first published in Paris. At the time that Shimazu Nariakira is supposed to have taken his self-portrait (1841), he was thirty-two years old. How odd it is that this thirty-two-year-old appears to be a man in his late forties or early fifties.

Reference to perhaps the earliest amateur photography in Japan appeared during 1859–60 in a long series of articles published in the *Photographic News* (London). The pieces tell of the experiences of a Norwegian traveler/photographer who was the first European to penetrate the interior of Japan in over a quarter of a century, and the first photographer to travel freely in the countryside. From the time of the Spanish and Portuguese expulsion from Japan in the 1630s, no European had been allowed to move without supervision in the interior. Thus, the peregrinations of this Norwegian (who chose to remain anonymous in order to protect his Japanese friends from government reprisals) are even more remarkable. If he had been caught, it would have meant death for him and his companions. Briefly, he arrived in Nagasaki in 1857 and was employed at the Dutch factory at Deshima. One day, while photographing in the streets of Nagasaki, he met a merchant-official, named Dsetjuma (a pseudonym), who took great interest in his work. Some days later, this Japanese man offered the Norwegian a position in his household so that he himself could learn photography. Abandoning European dress, the Norwegian adopted the Japanese mode and began to grow his hair so he could fix it in the style of the samurai. With a weakened photographic solution of silver nitrate, he dyed his skin a dark brown and then began plotting how he could satisfy his desire to see those parts of Japan that had remained hidden from European view. His strategy was to travel in reversed positions—with Dsetjuma affecting the role of photographer and himself that of assistant. Since the Norwegian did not speak idiomatic Japanese he feigned deafness on those occasions when people tried to draw him into conversation.

This incredible adventure lasted several months, and included an account of a ritual seppuku (a suicide), a description of the life and customs of the Japanese countryside, a visit to a Japanese court of justice, a trip to a porcelain factory, and encounters with a succession of venal Japanese priests. But perhaps just as fascinating as the social history related in the Norwegian's diaries are his observations concerning the first documented attempt by a Japanese amateur to make a photograph.

> I was taking a turn around the garden when I came on Dsetjuma in the act of fixing the tent.... I did not interfere in the operation at all, being interested in seeing what sort of a result he would obtain without assistance....[The first attempt to make a negative a failure, Dsetjuma tried another plate.] A second attempt, in which I assisted him, being more successful he recovered his spirits...he could not resist giving himself the pleasure of taking it outside and showing it to his countrymen. Loud were their expressions of admiration..."[19]

About perspective as the Japanese perceived it, the Norwegian offered these comments.

> I found that nothing surprised and interested the Japanese so much as these pictures....Evidently, they regarded both of us as practicers of magical arts, and I did not think the worse of their understandings....What used to puzzle them considerably—and I am not speaking of the middle and lower classes only—was the perspective. A man in the distance they thought a little boy, because he was so much smaller than a man in the foreground....It was, no doubt, owing to this that they never seemed so much impressed by looking at a photograph of a landscape as at a representation of a house or a temple or a group of horses or men.[20]

Amateur interest in photography flourished in the late 1850s and extended to the highest levels of Japanese official society—the daimyo (the territorial baron of feudal Japan) and the immediate family of the last Tokugawa shogun. Albums in the possession of Tokugawa Yoshinobu (a lineal descendant of the last shogun) contain hundreds of photographs of this period taken by the brother of Keiki (the last shogun). During the 1870s and first half of the 1880s, amateur interest subsided, but in the mid-1880s George Eastman succeeded in manufacturing easy-to-use dry plates that vastly simplified photography. The result was a universal quickening of interest in the medium; in Japan amateur photography was a fad that caught on.

· In 1887, an Englishman arrived in Japan and almost single-handedly changed the course of amateur interest in photography. William Kinnimond Burton, expatriate professor of sanitary engineering, was the most popular writer in the world on the subject of technical photography (*The ABC of Modern Photography*, *Burton's Modern Photography*), and his presence in Japan galvanized photographic activity.

In 1889, Burton was instrumental in founding the Japanese Photographic Society, serving as one of its first secretaries. The Society became an instant public success, attracting the leaders of Tokyo society, as well as an impressive cross section of photographers working in Japan. Its culminating achievement occurred in 1893, when it sponsored the first international photographic exhibition in Japan, which brought to Tokyo 296 photographs done by members of the Camera Club of London. The purpose of the exhibition was to introduce the best amateur work being done in Europe at the time, but its extraordinary popular success and great critical acclaim indicated that the interest in photography extended well beyond its practitioners to include the Japanese public.

Perhaps the most avid amateur practitioner of photography in Japan during the 1890s was a friend of both Ogawa and Burton named Kajima Seibei. A wealthy Tokyo merchant, Kajima probably provided the financial backing for many of Ogawa's projects, and indeed, spent so much time pursuing his hobby that his own businesses went into bankruptcy. The *Journal of the Photographic Society of India* reviewed Kajima's work at an exhibition in Calcutta.

[Included in a group of photographs sent by Professor Burton]...came a collection of fans of various sizes and shapes, flowers, birds, etc., and printed in silver. These are the handiwork of Mr. Kajima, whom Professor Burton describes as the most enthusiastic amateur in Japan, and who certainly possesses in no small degree the artistic feeling so characteristic of these clever people. There are also two indescribable articles of clothing, very artistically decorated [by Mr. Kajima] with photographs printed on silver on silk. One of these is the *obi*...the other is the *haori* (which corresponds to the ordinary frock coat worn by Europeans).[21]

This idiosyncratic and marvelous application of photography can serve as a concluding symbol of how the Japanese invested an art form introduced by the West with the stamp of their own artistic traditions.

Since the nineteenth century, appreciation for topographical photography has been eclipsed by a fascination with individual stylists. In the last few years, however, there has been a renewed interest in rediscovering the work of photographers who not only created works of artistic merit, but also documented periods of history in a comprehensive way. In Japanese photography we find the greatest range of subjects and the most detailed look at daily life, cultural heritage, social preoccupations, landscape, and all other aspects of life in a medieval society. Although influenced by Europeans, this body of work retains a freshness and originality that differentiate it from other Asian photographs. The painstaking tradition of hand-tinting prints, the mixture of dramatic and serene compositions, the close resemblance (in styles and content) to the ukiyo-e prints all combine to give nineteenth-century photography in Japan a special place in the larger continuum of Japanese art.

Clark Worswick

Notes

1. Raja Lala Deen Dayal, photographer by appointment to H.H. the Nizam of Hyderabad (India) and Afong Lai of Hong Kong were two notable exceptions to the rule.

2. Though Hawks is listed as author of this work, Perry supervised the elaborate production of the three volumes that comprised the official report entitled *Narrative of the Expedition of an American Squadron to the China Seas and Japan, Performed in the Years 1852, 1853 and 1854 Under the Command of Commodore M. C. Perry, United States Navy* (Washington, 1856). The report was printed in a huge edition of 18,000; the government bore the $360,000 cost. For more information on Brown and this work see William Elliot Griffis, *Matthew Calbraith Perry* (Boston: Houghton, Mifflin & Co., 1890), p. 385.

3. William Welling, *Photography in America: The Formative Years* (New York: T. Y. Crowell, 1978), p. 120.

4. Sir Rutherford Alcock, *The Capital of the Tycoon* (London: Longman, Green, 1863), p. 68.

5. Laurence Oliphant, *Episodes in a Life of Adventure* (London: William Blackwood & Sons, 1888), p. 195.

6. Pat Barr, in *The Coming of the Barbarians* (London: Macmillan, 1967), p. 134, mentions Gower: "Gower one of the young secretaries had been trying to develop some of the photos he had taken during the journey." It is mainly supposed that Gower was the photographer of the Negretti & Zambra series, because no other reference to European photographers working in Tokyo (Edo) during 1861 has been found. The series of photographs published by Negretti & Zambra was used in Thos. Clarke Westfield, *The Japanese—Their Manners & Customs* (London, 1862), and in George Smith, *Ten Weeks in Japan* (London, 1861). Gower's last official appearance in Japan was in the mid-1860s, when he was sent to Hokkaido to replace a consular officer who had been implicated in looting Ainu graveyards. In European anthropological circles, a whole female Ainu skeleton brought up to $2,000.

7. In mid-1864 Ernest Satow, then a young student interpreter (later British minister to Peking), met Beato aboard the flagship of the Shimonoseki expedition, the *Euryalus*; his observations suggest that Beato had been resident in the country some months before the expedition. "The only civilian on board was Felix Beato, the well-known photographer, who, making his first start in life with a camera in the Crimean war...had subsequently settled in Japan, where his social qualities had gained him many friends." *A Diplomat in Japan* (Philadelphia: J. B. Lippincott & Co., 1921), p. 102.

8. References to Beato's commercial activities can be found in *The Chronicle & Directory for China, Japan, the Philippines, and the Straits Settlements* for the period 1868–84. (The most complete set of this valuable research work is in the Hong Kong University library.) On Feb. 6, 1877, *The Daily Press* (Hong Kong) carried the following notice: "...sold stock and good will of photographic business, 17 Bund to Messrs. Stillfried and Andersen, F. Beato, Yokohama, Jan. 23."

9. Aimé Humbert quoted by Bayard Taylor in *Japan in Our Day* (New

York: Charles Scribner's Sons, 1892), p. 111. Humbert's descriptions first appeared in French in his work *Japon Illustré* (Paris: Corbeil, 1870), in which woodcuts made from Beato's photographs are used extensively.

10. Ibid., p. 113.

11. An album in the possession of the British Ambassador, Tokyo, lists pre-fire photographs available from Signor F. Beato: "Japan Albums Complete $200., Japan half albums $100., Views of Japan $2., Levant $2., China $2., India $2., Cartes de visite $15. per doz., 2nd doz. $10., Large Portrait 7 x 9...$15., Large Portrait 10 x 15...$25."

12. Wirgman was perhaps the most influential Western artist resident in Japan during the Meiji period. His students included Japanese artists who took up painting in the Western mode among whom were: Takahashi Yuichi, Goseda Yoshimatsu, Yamomoto Hosui, Kobori Seigan (who adapted woodblock printing to the Western style), and Tamura Shuritsu.

13. *Photographic News* (London), 1866, p. 48.

14. *Photographic News* (London), Feb. 29, 1884, p. 124.

15. The best compilation of names, dates, and a miscellany of general Japanese photographic information is contained in *Nippon Sashin Shi* (Tokyo: Heibonsha, 1971). Mr. Hiroaki Sato kindly translated the chronology section at the end of this work for me into English. While this book is the premier effort in Japanese on the subject of nineteenth-century photography, I personally remain baffled at where the information came from as there is no footnoting in the book.

16. Pierre Loti, *Madame Chrysanthème* (Tokyo: Charles E. Tuttle, 1973), pp. 250-252.

17. *Journal of the Photographic Society of India*, June, 1891, p. 91.

18. *Modern Photography*, May, 1976, p. 62.

19. *Photographic News* (London), October 28, 1859, p. 92.

20. *Photographic News* (London), January 27, 1860, p. 250.

21. *Journal of the Photographic Society of India*, June, 1891, p. 91.

Description of
Photographic Processes

CALOTYPE (TALBOTYPE): The first negative/positive process—patented by William Henry Fox Talbot (February 1841). In the calotype process a negative image was produced by sensitizing writing paper with chemical solutions. After an exposure of two to three minutes, the negative was developed. The process was then repeated with a fresh piece of paper sandwiched against the negative; this produced a positive print. The advantage of the process was that several positives could be struck from a single negative.

DAGUERREOTYPE: The first photographic process to enjoy popular success—invented by Louis Daguerre and given "free to the world" by the French Government (August 1839). The daguerreotype was a direct positive made on a sensitized metal plate, which was exposed for fifteen to twenty minutes. Since no negative was used in the process, each daguerreotype was a single, unique photograph.

DRY PLATE PROCESS: A negative photographic process in which gelatin replaced wet collodion as the emulsion on the glass plate. Introduced commercially in 1873, the dry plate process superseded the wet collodion process, as dry plates could be purchased already prepared and could be stored for long periods of time.

WET PLATE (WET COLLODION) PROCESS: A negative photographic process invented by Frederick Scott Archer (1851). The process took its name from the fact that a sensitized glass plate was exposed in the camera while it was still wet. The negative then had to be developed on the spot after an exposure of two to three seconds. The advantage of the process was that the photographer could see his picture almost immediately; the disadvantage was that preparing the plate for exposure required erecting a portable darkroom, mixing chemicals, and developing the plate, many times in difficult circumstances. Additionally, the wet-plate photographer needed large amounts of hard-to-find fresh water, not to mention the fact that his equipment oftentimes literally weighed tons.

Print Processes

ALBUMEN PRINT: The most popular photographic printing paper in use during the nineteenth century. Introduced by L. D. Blanquart-Evrard in 1850, by 1860 it was manufactured by a variety of firms some of which used as many as 60,000 eggs a day to obtain the albumen (egg white) used as the binder of the paper.

CARTE-DE-VISITE: Popularized by Andre Disdéri in the mid-1850s, the format was originally conceived as a photographic visiting card and usually measured 65 by 90 mm. During the 1860s the popularity of the 'carte' was such that in London alone over two hundred photographers specialized in them.

COLLOTYPE: An early *photo-mechanical* printing process invented by Alphonse Poitevin in 1855. In the process a glass plate was coated with gelatin and sensitized; when the plate was inked and printed, it produced prints with finely reticulated grain and a delicate chiaroscuro.

SILVER BROMIDE PRINT: Introduced in the early 1880s, the bromide print is the most widely used type of paper print today. The paper is coated with a gelatin emulsion containing silver iodide and silver bromide.

STEREOSCOPIC PRINT: A binocular print mounted on a rigid card. Developed in 1838 by Sir Charles Wheatstone, stereos became widely popular after the Great Exhibition of 1851. In the process two almost identical photographs were taken from a slightly different point of view; they were then mounted side by side on a card and when viewed through a binocular device they created the illusion of a three-dimensional view.

Hand Coloring

During the nineteenth century—by the 1880s—it was an almost obligatory practice among Japanese photographers to hand color both studio and landscape pictures. In Europe the practice of tinting photographs fell into almost universal disrepute, but in Japan, because of the consummate skill of the Japanese watercolorist (the medium of tinting), hand-colored albumen photographs became a minor art form of startling beauty. The process of coloring a photograph was infinitely tedious, and a master colorist could be expected to produce two or three finished prints during a twelve-hour day. Some photographs required a master to color them—where individual faces among hundreds in a crowd scene had to be "worked up" (page 22) or where particular rocks in a Japanese garden each had to be given their own individual tones and textures (page 79). During 1889, A. Farsari, a commercial photographer of Yokohama, employed fifteen painters to hand color his photographs, and these far outnumbered the other craftsmen in the studio.

Index of Commercial and Amateur Photographers in Japan, 1854-1905

AMATA GUAN

Commercial, 1880s, Odawara; later became itinerant photographer.

ANDERSEN, H.

Commercial, 1875(?)–85, Yokohama; partner in Stillfried & Andersen/the Japan Photographic Association, which bought the studio and stock of Felix Beato, January 1877.

ANDREW, W. P.

Commercial, 1868, Yokohama.

ANTHONY, E. & H. T.

Commercial, 1862, New York; published 5 stereos of Views of Japan.

BEASLEY, F.

Amateur, 1875.

BEATO, FELIX

Commercial, 1864–85, Yokohama; Beato, Saunders, and Stillfried were the most important European photographers of nineteenth-century Japan; sold negatives and custom to Stillfried, January 23, 1877.

BEATO & WIRGMAN

Commercial artists and photographers, 1865–69, Yokohama; the original partnership that brought Beato to Japan; early negatives probably burned in Yokohama fire of 1866.

BELCHER, H. W.

Amateur, 1890s; photographs used in W. Weston, *Mountaineering and Exploring in the Japanese Alps* (London: Murray, 1896).

BLACK, JOHN REDDIE

Editor, *The Far East* (Yokohama, 1870–75), the first photographically illustrated periodical published in Japan.

BRINKLEY, CAPT. F.

Editor, *Japan Described and Illustrated by the Japanese* (Boston: Millet, 1897–98), at least 5 editions, most containing tipped-in photographs; editor, *Japan: Its History, Arts, and Literature* (1901).

BROWN, ELIPHALET, JR.

Official photographer, Acting Master's Mate, Perry Expedition, Japan, 1853–54; the first European to photograph in Japan.

BURTON, PROF. WILLIAM KINNIMOND

Amateur, 1887–99, Tokyo; photographer and prolific writer on photographic techniques, a guiding light of the *Photographic Society of Japan*, he was also a silent partner in Ogawa's collotype establishment.

DOUGLAS, J.

Commercial, 1884, Yokohama.

DSETJUMA

Amateur, 1857–59, Nagasaki; Japanese merchant/official who was the employer/student of the Norwegian.

ENAMI N.

Commercial, 1890s–1919, Yokohama.

ENDO MATSUO

Official photographer, Kurile Islands Expeditionary Team, 1892.

ENOMOTO TAKEAKI, VISCOUNT

Amateur, 1889–(?) President of the *Photographic Society of Japan*, Ambassador to China and Russia, Minister of Education, Communication, Foreign Affairs, and Member of the Privy Council.

EZAKI KIYOSHI

Amateur, 1880s; son of Ezaki Reiji, returned from U.S. after three years of study, demonstrated enlarging and flash equipment.

EZAKI REIJI

Commercial, 1880s; one of the first "snapshot photographers" to use dry plates in Japan, succeeded in photographing total eclipse of the sun, mine explosions, etc. Made collage of 1,700 photographs of babies and used it for an advertisement.

FAIRWEATHER, ANGUS

Amateur, 1866–67: groups, landscapes, and architecture produced from small-sized negatives.

FARSARI, A., & CO.

Commercial, 1886–1924, Yokohama; acquired partial stock of the Japan Photographic Association/Stillfried & Co./ Stillfried & Andersen, which, in 1877, had acquired the stock of Felix Beato/ Beato & Wirgman. The most prolific of all commercial photographic firms in Japan, Farsari specialized in albums of tinted views.

FRITH OF REIGATE
Commercial, 1892, England; the *Catalogue of Frith of Reigate* lists "One Hundred views of China & Japan...including nine very curious illustrations of Japanese temple worship" by an unattributed photographer.

FUKATANI KOMAKICHI
Amateur, 1900; active in China during the Boxer Rebellion.

FUKAZAWA YOKITSU
Editor and equipment manufacturer, 1870s–1880s; published *Sashin Zasshi*, the first Japanese photographic periodical.

FUKUYAMAKAN ARTISTIC
PHOTOGRAPHIC STUDIO
Commercial, 1890s, Tokyo; Narita T., manager.

GENROKUKAN
Commercial photography studio run by Kajima Kiyosaburo, 1895–1916(?), Tokyo.

GORDES, A.
Commercial, 1888, Nagasaki.

GORDES, H.
Commercial, 1888, Nagasaki.

GOWER
Amateur, 1861; accompanied British Minister Alcock, on trip from Nagasaki to Edo (Tokyo); present during attack on legation; work published by Negretti & Zambra as "Views of Japan."

HAMILTON, H. J.
Amateur, 1890s; photographs used in W. Weston, *Mountaineering and Exploring in the Japanese Alps* (London: Murray, 1896).

HORI T.
Amateur, 1890s; photographs used in W. Weston, *Mountaineering and Exploring in the Japanese Alps* (London: Murray, 1896).

HORIE HIKOJIRO
Amateur, 1860s, Tokyo; with Uyeno Hikoma photographed the Todo family in Tokyo.

ICHIDA S.
Commercial, 1890s; photographs used in W. Weston, *Mountaineering and Exploring in the Japanese Alps* (London: Murray, 1896).

ICHIDA SOTA
Commercial, 1870, Hyogo.

ISAWA I.
Amateur, 1890, Tokyo; demonstrated his work with micro-photographs to the Photographic Society of Japan.

ISIYAMA OOME
Commercial, 1870s–1880s.

JAMES, M.
Commercial, 1875, Yokohama.

JAPAN PHOTOGRAPHIC ASSOCIATION
Commercial, 1875(?)–1885, Yokohama; successor to Stillfried & Andersen/Stillfried & Co.; in 1877 purchased stock and custom of Felix Beato/Beato & Wirgman; in 1886–87 the company was sold to Kusakabe Kimbei and to A. Farsari, Yokohama.

KAJIMA & SUWO
Commercial, 1900s, Tokyo.

KAJIMA KIYOSABURO
Commercial, 1895–1916(?), Tokyo; younger brother of Kajima Seibei; operated Genrokukan, the most lavish commercial establishment in Japan, published *The Ainu of Japan*, illustrated with photographs.

KAJIMA SEIBEI
Amateur, 1890s, Tokyo; fanatically devoted amateur, once Tokyo's richest merchant, founding member of the Photographic Society of Japan, helped finance Ogawa's collotype establishment, photographed Kabuki.

KAJIMA SEIBEI, JR.
Amateur, 1890s, Tokyo; son of Kajima Seibei, elected member of Photographic Society of Japan, 1894.

KAMEYA TOKUJIRO
Commercial, 1868, Nagasaki; operated a shajo (open air studio).

KAMEYA TOYO

Commercial, 1868, Nagasaki; the first Japanese woman in photography, operated a shajo with her father Kameya Tokujiro.

KAWASAKI MICHITAMI

Amateur, 1860s; physician to the diplomatic mission that toured Europe in 1862; while in Europe he studied photography.

KITAINIWA TSUKUBA

Commercial, 1871, Okuyama, Asakusa.

KIZU KOKICHI

Commercial, 1864, Hakodate; taught photography by the first Russian consul, Goskevich; opened first studio in Hokkaido.

KONDO T.

Amateur, 1890s, Tokyo; at the Photographic Society of Japan demonstrated carbon paper made by the Autotype Co. of London.

KONOYE T., MARQUIS

Amateur, 1890s, Tokyo; Vice President the Photographic Society of Japan, 1893.

KUMAGAYA SHIN

Amateur, 1874, Formosa; self-appointed photographer to the Japanese Army, accompanied Taiwan Expedition, killed by stray bullet, 1874.

KUSAKABE KIMBEI

Commercial, 1880s–1912, Yokohama; bought major portion of Japan Photographic Association/Stillfried & Co.

KUWATA SHOZABURO

Commercial, 1875–1900(?), Kyoto/Osaka.

LE BAS, A.

Amateur, 1860s, Yokohama/Shimonoseki.

LEWIS, KARL

Commercial, 1900s–1915(?), Yokohama.

MARUKI R.

Commercial, 1880s.

MATSUZAKI SHINJI

Commercial, 1870s; photographed Ogasawara Islands (1872), Taiwan Expedition (1874), articles of Japanese manufacture (1877).

MILLER, M.

Commercial, 1860–64, Hong Kong; *New Catalogue of Stereoscopes and Views*, E. & H. T. Anthony (1862), lists 5 stereos of Japan, probably by Miller.

MIYAUCHI KOTARO

Amateur, 1900, Tokyo; founder of Toyo Sashin Kyo (the Oriental Photographic Society), a school of artistic photography that attempted to produce painting-like effects in photography.

MIZUNO H.

Commercial, 1891, Yokohama; perhaps one of the last daguerreotypists operating in the world, Mizuno also invented lacquer photographs.

MORITA RAIZO

Commercial, 1865, Koraibashi, Osaka; set up a shajo (an outdoor photographic studio) the first of its kind in Japan.

MOSER, MICHAEL

Commercial, 1870s, Yokohama; photographer for the *Far East* magazine.

MURATA SEIUNDO

Amateur, 1876; photographed the Hagi rebellion (1876).

NAKAHAMA MANJIRO

Amateur, 1860s; member of the first shogunal diplomatic mission (to the U.S.), he studied photography while in America.

NEGRETTI & ZAMBRA

Commercial, 1850s; commissioned Rossier's trip to China (1857–59); published first commercial views of Japan, as a stereo series (1861), taken by Gower.

THE NORWEGIAN

Amateur, 1857–59, Nagasaki; traveled in disguise through Japan before it was open to foreigners, took photographs with Dsetjuma, his employer, a merchant/official; diaries published anonymously in the *Photographic News* (1859) are the first account of photography in Japan.

J. NUMASHIMA'S FINE ART EXHIBITION

Commercial, 1890s, Yokohama.

ODA NOBUSATO

Amateur, 1859, daimyo of Tendo.

OGAWA ISSHIN
Commercial, 1880–1918(?), Tokyo; with Kusakabe the outstanding Japanese photographer of the nineteenth and early twentieth centuries.

OGURA K.
Official photographer, 1890s, the Laboratory of the Army and Navy Staff; member of the Photographic Society of Japan, photographed Sino-Japanese War, 1895.

OKABE, VISCOUNT
Amateur, Vice President of the Photographic Society of Japan.

OMURA, COUNT
Amateur, 1893, member of the Photographic Society of Japan.

OSHIMA KEN'ICHI
Official photographer, 1886; published *Gun'yo Kogeigaku Kyotei* (Manual of Military Craftsmanship: Military Photography) as a textbook for the Japanese Military Academy, later Lt. General; Minister of the Army.

PARANT, C.
Commercial, 1872, Yokohama; painter and photographer, who worked in 1872/73, also, for Baron von Stillfried.

POINTING, HERBERT
Commercial, 1901–6; first came to Japan on a tour for *Leslie's Weekly* (1901); returned intermittently until 1906; published *Fuji-San* (25 pictures); *Japanese Studies* (52 pictures), *Camera Pictures in the Far East; In Lotus Land Japan* (2 editions: 1910, 1922).

RAU, W. H.
Commercial, 1900s, Philadelphia; toured Japan, his photographs appeared in D. C. Angus, *Japan: The Eastern Wonderland* (London: Cassel & Co., 1904).

SAUNDERS. W.
Commercial, November 1862, Yokohama; based in Shanghai 1864–88, Saunders did important early work in Japan, used by *Illustrated London News*, 1863, pp. 256, 261–62; perhaps most underrated photographer of Far Asia.

SHIBATA TSUNEKICHI
Amateur, 1900; Boxer Rebellion, China.

SHIMAZU NARIAKIRA, LORD
Amateur, 1840(?)–58(?).

SHIMOOKA RENJO
Commercial, 1859(?)–1900s, Yokohama; the grand old man and the longest-lived Japanese commercial photographer (1859–1914).

STILLFRIED & ANDERSEN
Commercial, 1875(?)–85, Yokohama; same firm as Japan Photographic Association; stock sold to Kusakabe Kimbei.

STILLFRIED & CO.
Commercial, 1871–75, Yokohama.

STILLFRIED, BARON VON
Commercial, 1871–85, Yokohama; Baron R. von Stillfried Rateniz operated Stillfried & Co. (1871–75), Japan Photographic Association/Stillfried & Andersen (1875–85); in 1877 the firm bought Felix Beato's stock and custom and moved into his studio; major portion of stock sold to Kusakabe Kimbei.

SUGAWARA C.
Commercial, 1889–1915(?), Yokohama; chief operator, A. Farsari & Co.

SUTTON, F. W.
Amateur, 1868, Yokohama.

SUZUI S.
Commercial, 1905, Yokohama.

SUZUKI SHIN'ICHI
Commercial, 1865–1890s(?), Tokyo; student of Shimooka Renjo (1865), elected to Photographic Society of Japan (1891).

TAKEBAYASHI SEICHI
Commercial, 1870s, Yokohama; assistant to Baron von Stillfried, hired by commissioner of land development to photograph Konno, Harushige.

TAMAGAWA SANJI
Commercial, 1865, Tokyo; set up a shajo (an open air studio); known as the most successful photographer in Tokyo in the mid-1860s.

TAMAMOTO KENZO
Commercial, 1869s–70s, Hakodate; hired by commissioner of land development (Hokkaido) to photograph Sapporo, Otaru, Hakodate.

TAMAMURA K.
Commercial, 1880–1912, Yokohama; one of the most successful commercial photographers of the late nineteenth century and a rival of both Kusakabe and of A. Farsari & Co.; published *A Leaf From the Diary of a Young Lady*, *Famous Scenes in Japan*.

TAMEMASA
Commercial, 1880s–1915(?), Nagasaki; specialized in "views and costumes of Japan."

TAMOTO K.
Commercial, 1880s, Hakodate.

TODA T., COUNT
Amateur, 1892, Tokyo; Vice President of the Photographic Society of Japan.

TOKUGAWA ATSUNORI, PRINCE
Amateur, 1893, Tokyo; Vice President of the Photographic Society of Japan.

TOMISHIGE RIHEI
Commercial, 1866, Chikugo/Kumamoto; a protege of Uenyo Hikoma, he later operated his own studios.

TOSHIAKI KAMEI, COUNT
Official photographer, 1890s, Sino-Japanese war; accompanied 2nd Army during war with five personal servants, fifteen porters; brought out in 1897 *Meiji 27-8 Nen Sen'Eki Sashincho* (photographic album of the conflicts in the 27th and 28th years of Meiji).

UCHIDA KYUICHI
Commercial, 1859–75, Osaka/Yokohama; with Shimooka and Uyeno a major figure in early Japanese photography; 1872, photographed the Emperor Meiji.

UYENO HIKOMA
Commercial, 1860–90s, Tokyo/Nagasaki/Hong Kong/Shanghai; with Ogawa, Kusakabe, Uchida and Shimooka, a major figure in nineteenth-century Japanese photography.

UYENO KOMA
Commercial, 1872, Tokyo; assisted Uchida in photographing the Emperor Meiji.

UYENO TOSHINOJO
Amateur, 1840s, Nagasaki; a wealthy merchant chemist, reputedly imported the first daguerreotype camera into Japan (1840) which he gave/sold to Lord Shimazu; the father of Uyeno Hikoma, Uyeno Koma.

WEST, C. D.
Amateur, 1880s–90s, Tokyo; founding member of the Photographic Society of Japan and leading amateur of the period.

WHITE, H. C. & CO.
Commercial, 1900s. Brought out stereo series of Japan; Pointing was contributor to series.

WIRGMAN, CHARLES
Commercial, 1862–70, Yokohama; artist for the *London Illustrated News*, he undoubtedly influenced Beato to come to Japan; partner in Beato & Wirgman (1865–69); imprisoned with Beato in libel action in Yokohama jail during late 1860s; publisher/artist *The Japan Punch*.

YAMAMOTO SANSHICHIRO
Commercial, 1890–1916(?), Tokyo/Peking; elected Photographic Society of Japan, 1893; resident of Peking during the Boxer Rebellion.

YEGI M.
Commercial, 1890s, Tokyo; elected to the Photographic Society of Japan, 1893.

YOKOYAMA MATSUSABURO
Commercial, 1860s–80s, Ryogoku/Tokyo; student of Shimooka; commissioned by the Ninagawa Shikitane to photograph art objects (1870); lecturer in photography and lithography at the Japanese Military Academy until 1881; from 1882 onwards devoted himself to "photographic oil paintings."

Members of the Photographic Society of Japan, 1890s
(Partial list of membership—171 members, 1893)

Officers

Viscount Enomoto, *President of the Society*
Viscount Okabe, *Vice President*
Marquis Tokugawa A., *Vice President*
Prince Konoye T., *Vice President*
Count Toda T., *Vice President*
W. K. Burton, *Vice President*
Prof. J. Scriba, *Vice President*
Prof. John Milne, F.R.S., *Vice President*

Members

d'Anethan, Baron A.	Henry, G.	Le Poer Trench, P.	Rokujo M.
Arito K.	Holmes, Edmund R.	Longford, Joseph	Sato K.
Baehr, H.	Hornell, E. A.	Macnab, A. F.	Shand, W. J. S.
Beitter, E.	Ichioka T.	Marx, E.	Sharpe, H. T.
Block, E.	Isawa I.	Mason, W. B.	Shimooka R.
Brikworth, G.	Ishikawa I.	Munster, B.	Suyenbobo M.
Brower, L.	Kajima S.	Nakahara M.	Suzuki S.
Date, M.	Kajima S., Jr.	Narahara K.	Tanabe S., Prof.
Detrich, Prof.	Kamiya T.	Naruta T.	Tanaka I.
Divers (F.R.S.), Dr. E.	Kanda N.	Nonogaki S.	Tatsuke K.
Duff, C. M.	Kano	Ogawa K.	Vander Heyden, W.
Forbes, Capt. W. H.	Keil O.	Ogura K.	West, C. D.
Gordon, W.	Kikkawa S.	Omura, Count	Yamamoto S.
Hamilston, R.	Kikuchi D., Prof.	Otsuki C.	Yashiki Kaga
Hasegawa T.	Kiyokawa T.	Pigott, H. C.	Yegi M.
Heckert, H.	Konishi T.	Pineyro, T. V.	Yesaki K.
	Lenze, Dr. A.	Ricketts, J.	

Bibliography

Alcock, Sir Rutherford, *The Capital of the Tycoon* (London: Longman, Green, 1863).

Barr, Pat, *The Coming of the Barbarians* (London: Macmillan, 1967).

Barr, Pat, *The Deer Cry Pavilion* (London: Macmillan, 1968).

Cameron, Nigel, *From Bondage to Liberation* (Hong Kong: Oxford University Press, 1975).

Chamberlain, Basil Hall, *Things Japanese* (London: K. Paul, Trench, Trubner & Co. Ltd., 1890).

De Becker, J. E., *The Nightless City* (Tokyo: Charles E. Tuttle, 1971).

Dunn, Charles J., *Traditional Japan* (Tokyo: Charles E. Tuttle, 1972).

Griffis, William Elliott, *Matthew Calbraith Perry* (Boston: Houghton, Mifflin & Co., 1890).

Hall, John Whitney, *Japan: From Prehistory to Modern Times* (New York: Delacorte Press, 1968).

Loti, Pierre, *Madame Chrysanthème* (Tokyo: Charles E. Tuttle, 1973).

Nippon Sashin Shi (Tokyo: Heibonsha, 1971).

Oliphant, Laurence, *Episodes in a Life* (London: William Blackwood & Sons, 1888).

Papinot, E., *Historical and Geographical Dictionary of Japan* (Tokyo: Charles E. Tuttle, 1974).

Rosenfield, John M., *Tradition and Modernization in Japanese Culture* (Princeton: The Conference on Modern Japan of the Association for Asian Studies, Inc./The Princeton University Press, 1971).

Satow, Sir Ernest, *A Diplomat in Japan* (Philadelphia: J. B. Lippincott & Co., 1921).

Shibusawa Keizo, ed., *Japanese Life and Culture in the Meiji Era* (Tokyo: The Toyo Bunko, 1969).

Szarkowski, John, and Yamagishi Shoji, eds., *New Japanese Photography* (New York: The Museum of Modern Art/New York Graphic Society, 1974).

Taylor, Bayard, *Japan in Our Day* (New York: Charles Scribner's Sons, 1892).

Von Siebold, Dr. Philipp Franz, *Manners and Customs of the Japanese* (Tokyo: Charles E. Tuttle, 1973).

Worswick, Clark, and Jonathan Spence, *Imperial China* (New York, Pennwick/Crown, 1978).

Picture Sources

Lawrence & Martha Friedricks, New York: 18, 20, 21, 23, 26, 49, 50, 53, 57, 58, 66, 74, 79, 90, 106, 109, 110, 113, 115, 123, 126.

The Library of Congress, Washington, D.C.: 30, 68-70, 81

Harry Lunn, Jr., Graphics International, Washington, D.C.: 14, 16, 17, 19, 27, 28, 31, 32, 38, 48, 50, 54-56, 61, 77, 82, 88, 89, 91-95.

Peabody Museum of Salem, Massachusetts: 100, 101, 111.

Arthur & Marilyn Penn, New York: 1, 2, 33-36, 40, 59, 64, 72, 73, 75, 83, 98, 108, 112, 114, 122, 124, 125.

Howard & Jane Ricketts, London: 46, 52, 62, 76, 96, 97, 99, 101, 103, 104, 105.

The National Museum of Natural History, The Smithsonian Institution, Washington, D.C.: 15, 42-44, 116-119.

Private Collections: 12, 22, 24, 41, 60, 63, 65, 67, 78, 80, 84–86, 102, 107, 120, 121, 127.

This book was designed by Michael Flanagan